Two Wheels A'Blazing

Register This New Book

Benefits of Registering

- ✓ FREE accidental damage replacements
- ✓ FREE audio book – *Pilgrim's Progress*, audiobook edition
- ✓ FREE information about new titles and other freebies

www.anekopress.com/new-book-registration

Two Wheels A'Blazing

Jesus Loves Bikers

Beth A. Mangus Roberts
Gal 2:20

BETH A. MANGUS ROBERTS

ANEKO
PRESS

We love hearing from our readers. Please contact us at www.anekopress.com/questions-comments with any questions, comments, or suggestions.

Visit Beth's website: www.christianriders.net

Two Wheels A'Blazing – Beth A. Mangus Roberts

Copyright © 2017

First edition published 2017

Cover Design: Natalia Hawthorne, BookCoverLabs.com

Cover Photography: Cattallina/Shutterstock

eBook Icon: Icons Vector/Shutterstock

Editors: Heather Thomas, Paul Miller, and Charlotte Graber

Printed in the United States of America

Aneko Press – *Our Readers Matter*™

www.anekopress.com

Aneko Press, Life Sentence Publishing, and our logos are trademarks of Life Sentence Publishing, Inc.

203 E. Birch Street

P.O. Box 652

Abbotsford, WI 54405

BIOGRAPHY & AUTOBIOGRAPHY / Religious

Paperback ISBN: 978-1-62245-370-2

eBook ISBN: 978-1-62245-371-9

10 9 8 7 6 5 4 3 2 1

Available where books are sold

Contents

To my Lord and Savior, Jesus Christ, who saved me from the pit of hell and then sent me on the adventure of a lifetime that has yet to end.

To D. Q. Roberts (DQ), my husband, best friend, ministry partner, favorite preacher, and soulmate. He always encouraged me to be my best. He challenged my faith, out-served me at every turn, and loved me completely, with unconditional love. He is the love of my life. When God put us together, He took two halves and united us as a whole; when DQ graduated to heaven, I became half a person again. DQ longed for me to publish this work, but sadly, he didn't see this day. Maybe God will give him a copy in heaven.

To everyone who has loved me, encouraged me, prayed for me, ministered to me, or allowed me to minister to you, I want you to know that you have helped shape my life, and I offer you a profound "Thank you."

Therefore, since we have so great a cloud of witnesses surrounding us, let us also lay aside every encumbrance, and the sin which so easily entangles us, and let us run with endurance the race that is set before us. (Hebrews 12:1 NASB)

Foreword

After much prayer, I began to write this book by logically starting at the beginning. I documented my birth and my relationships with my four siblings. I continued on through my life and wrote about the pain, the sorrow, the separation, and the desperation I felt as I grew older. I included the drug and alcohol abuse, the sexual and physical abuse, and the heartaches I caused others by my retaliation and rebellion. I wrote, and I sobbed. As I relived the years, my heart broke, not only because of the pain I had experienced, but more so because of the pain I had inflicted upon others. After several weeks of this, I was an emotional wreck. Satan was laughing his head off. He had managed to remind me of a past that Jesus had declared gone, and of sins that Jesus had washed away by His blood and death on the cross due to His great mercy, grace, and love.

This book doesn't contain that part of my story, though. I originally intended to include it, but God, in His will and wisdom, set me on a different course. Those painful memories and experiences that took me weeks to type were erased by my computer in only thirty seconds. Tears of disappointment freely flowed down my face as I stared at my blank computer screen.

I cried aloud, "I can't write it all down again. It hurt too badly, and I can't relive it again."

Then *the Voice* calmly spoke to me, as He often does, in a small yet insistent whisper. He said, "Jesus erased that past in an instant, the moment you repented, quicker than your computer can work. You can't bring back your past sins any more than you can bring back the words that were erased. You won't relive it, because you have been bought and paid for. It is finished."

This time, tears of joy, rather than tears of pain, rolled down my cheeks. Truly, I had been mistaken. I had thought that in order for people to understand me, I would have to write about my past. To my logical mind, the past made me the person I am today. The world might agree with that kind of logic, but they don't know the whole story. Jesus Christ has made me who and what I am today. Because of His death on the cross of Calvary and His resurrection, I have placed my faith in Jesus, and He has forever changed me. That is the theme of this book. That is the theme of my life. Let us begin.

Chapter 1

Here Am I, Send Me!

Then I heard the voice of the Lord saying, "Whom shall I send? And who will go for us?" And I said, "Here am I. Send me!" (Isaiah 6:8 NIV)

The date was September 29, 1991. As usual, DQ and I were early for the service at the First Christian Church of Bayonet Point. However, nothing was usual about that Sunday. My parents sat beside us in the pew. In order to be with us that day, they attended our home church instead of their own. It was difficult for me to concentrate on the message Pastor Mel preached.

My mind drifted back to when the whole thing started. The building program mantra had been, "Not equal gifts, but equal sacrifices." We had fasted and prayed for a month, but received no clear answer on what God wanted us to give. In frustration, DQ, my husband, decided to donate his Harley Davidson Shovel/Pan motorcycle.[1] The church leaders wouldn't accept it, though, claiming that God was going to use it in our lives. DQ said, "Not in my life, He's not. I would never go back

---

1 On the old Harleys, the first word describes the engine, a shovelhead, and the second term denotes the transmission, a panhead. Hence a Shovel/Pan.

to the biker world, where my worst failures lie and my greatest temptations exist!"

We knew that all we had was because of the Lord. God had allowed us to live near the canal in a house with a swimming pool. God had blessed us with my successful real estate career, our bikes, our 1965 Pontiac hot rod, and my business car. All of which, except for the mortgage, God allowed us to pay off in one year. That same year, we also paid off $17,000 in consumer debt. We had been faithful in giving our ten percent to God, and He had blessed us.

As our burden increased, we prayed, "Lord, we acknowledge that all our material goods are Yours, and we are only the caretakers. Our lives belong to You, so show us what to do." We told God that we would give everything to Him if He wanted it. DQ and I prayed together daily and with great conviction. Then the dreams and visions began. Every sermon we heard led us to the same conclusion: people were dying and going to hell, and we were doing nothing about it.

When we awoke, we shared our dreams with each other. Though they were different, they brought us to the same conclusion: we had a deep, heart-wrenching desire to help our lost and hurting brothers and sisters in the biker world. We tried to ignore that desire, but without success. We tried to rationalize why we couldn't give everything up, but the vision continued to haunt us. The vision was of a church tent set up at motorcycle events around the country in which we would proclaim the message of Jesus Christ to a lost and dying community. That vision consumed us. We couldn't sleep. We couldn't eat. We couldn't work.

Finally, in desperation, we went to Mike Winsor, our associate minister and the man who was discipling us. We were sure he would tell us that we (and our dreams) were crazy. He didn't. Mike patiently listened to us as we explained what we had seen and felt. Then he quietly said, "I will need to get the elders to pray about this for a season, and then I will get back to you." The season lasted a while, and we continued to dream and struggle with the enormity of the task.

Several months later, Mike came back with the elders' answer. Mike and the elders, along with Mel Gresham, the senior minister, felt that God had called us into full-time biker ministry. We stared at Mike dumbstruck and naively asked, "What does that mean?"

God soon showed us that it meant giving every part of our lives to Him. DQ and I continued to pray, and we concluded that we were supposed to sell everything we owned, so we could freely follow God in the ministry He was calling us to. We would need the money to be able to travel and pay for Bibles, gas, and food. We knew we couldn't take care of, or afford, a home and also be on the road. If we kept our house, we knew our hearts would soon long for home, and we didn't want to try to serve God with divided hearts.

We tested God to see if it was really His will for us to go. We put the house on the market to see if it would sell. The house sold within a week. And since I was both the listing and selling agent, we didn't have to pay a commission. We stood amazed and scared, terrified by the fact that God was totally serious in this calling.

We had yard sales every weekend. Slowly, we watched the material proof of our seven years of marriage carried off by strangers. As we stepped out in faith into this new ministry, we decided that God would have to provide for us. We would concentrate on doing His work and trust Him to provide. So we accepted what He brought us and what was offered to us as we sold our life and our memories. Our $2,000 sofa brought us $560, but it was going to be used by a missionary family home on furlough. We accepted the money and praised God for it.

Each Saturday morning, we carried more of our possessions out to the driveway to be bargained for and carried off by strangers. This went on for six weeks until our house was nearly empty.

A week after the house sold, God provided a 1978 school bus for us to drive to the biker events. It already had the seats removed, so all we had to do was fix up the inside. DQ and I differed in our vision for the inside of the bus. His vision was a mattress in one corner and a camping stove in the other. Whereas, I had a charming, but much more complicated, vision of what the inside of our new "home" should look like. I envisioned a pedestal queen bed with storage drawers underneath and a kitchen area complete with propane stove and refrigerator. Of course, we would also need a shower and a sink. DQ fought the idea for a while, but in the end, he accepted my ideas. I reminded him, "If mama ain't happy, ain't nobody happy," and "Happy wife, happy life" – especially living full-time in a 210-square-foot space.

DQ gently squeezed my hand, and my mind snapped back to the present as Pastor Melvin Gresham began the commissioning ceremony that would conclude with us being sent out as missionaries. Pastor Mel read from the Scriptures, and a responsive reading by the congregation followed. Soon, DQ and I were called forward. We were met at the front of the church by the elders. Just a few weeks earlier, those same leaders of the church gave their blessing to the birth of this biker ministry. And after much prayer, they felt led by the Lord to ordain us as missionaries.

They had a lengthy discussion about whether to ordain both of us or only DQ, since our church didn't usually ordain women. It was finally decided that if we were to be successful in this God-sized venture, we would both need to be ordained. As we knelt at the altar, the men laid their hands upon us and prayed. Suddenly, I felt as though the roof of the church was gone, and a huge beam of sunshine, a heavenly light, was shining down on us. I took a deep breath. My mind went to Jesus' baptism when the Holy Spirit descended upon Him like a dove. Could I possibly be feeling a bit of what Jesus had felt? As the men finished the prayer, the name of Jesus rang in my ears as it never had before. It was as if I was hearing it for the first time. I knew that Jesus had just become much more to me than I ever realized before. The anointing was so powerful. We were now marked by the Holy Spirit, and our lives would never again be our own. We floated back to our seats with radiant faces. God had truly poured His Holy Spirit upon us, and our lives would never be the same.

Chapter 2

Firsts

These twelve Jesus sent out with the following instructions: "Do not get any gold or silver or copper to take with you in your belts— no bag for the journey or extra shirt or sandals or a staff, for the worker is worth his keep. (Matthew 10:5, 9-10 NIV)

Unfortunately, there was no one to teach us how to effectively reach the biker community with the gospel of Jesus Christ. We very seldom encountered a Christian biker before our salvation, and the one we did encounter was timidly handing out tracts in an obscure location. I think our whole group gave him a tough time and laughed at him. Our senior pastor, Mel Gresham, felt that we should attend Florida Christian College in Kissimmee, Florida. He knew we would benefit from the knowledge, and he thought it would help our credibility. On the other hand, our associate pastor, Mike Winsor, was afraid that the purity of our witness might be ruined if we attended a Christian college. He didn't want us to become obnoxious Bible students who thought we knew everything.

Wanting to be sure we were following God and submitting

to our elders, we made an appointment with the dean of Florida Christian College. The night before our appointment, DQ and I discussed how we should dress. Since our bus had very little storage room, most of our regular clothes had been sold at the yard sales. We decided that since we were now missionaries to the bikers, we needed to dress as bikers. So we dressed in our biker attire.

In addition to his long, flowing hair, DQ wore a beaded necklace, huge turquoise rings on every finger, and spurs on his knee-high, steel-toed, engineer boots. I thought he looked fine. I was dressed as a biker, too, with three or four earrings in each ear, a nose ring, thick hair flowing down my back to the top of my jeans, turquoise rings on every finger including my thumbs, a primary chain belt (yes – a belt made from the primary chain of a motorcycle!), and jeans that were tucked into my knee-high laced boots. DQ grinned every time he looked at me. I guess I looked equally fine to him.

Off to the college we roared on the Harley Shovel/Pan. We were ready to meet the dean, but he was not ready to meet us. After an hour-long interview, in which he was speechless most of the time, he promised to get back to us after he had talked with his trustees. We learned later that as soon as we left, he called Pastor Mel and asked, "Are these two for real?" It seemed that we weren't typical Bible college students, and we would violate many of the dress-code rules if we attended as we were. Go figure. DQ's shoulder-length hair, multiple piercings, and arms full of tattoos did not fit their code. My nose ring was suspect as well. Women were required to wear dresses to the twice-weekly chapels, and I couldn't do that and ride in on the Harley, which was our main transportation.

We soon received the dean's answer. The trustees realized that making us fit their mold would render us useless in the scooter world where we would serve. They would allow us to attend Florida Christian College just as we were. That statement empowered us and made us look forward to the knowledge we would obtain at college.

We felt an urgency in our calling. The fire in our bones threatened to consume us. We couldn't wait four years to begin the biker ministry, but we could attend Florida Christian College every winter and do biker ministry during the rest of the year. So our course was laid out for us, and both ministers were happy. Mel was glad that we would attend classes, and Mike was happy that we would still have the purity of our witness. Now the question became, "How would we reach the bikers?" The courses we would take at college were about the Bible. That would be very useful, but the college didn't offer a *Biker 101* class in their curriculum. We knew that God had a call on our lives, but now that we were ordained ministers, what were we to do?

With Mike Winsor's agreement, we met with him three times a week for counseling and planning. Mike's challenging questions and heart-searching prayers led us to create Christian Riders Ministry (CRM). We prayed about the name, where we would go, how we would get there, what we would say, and how we would pay for it all. Mike challenged us to develop Bible lessons and get our one-, three-, and five-minute testimonies down pat. Slowly, day by day, CRM unfolded. As a child grows inside a mother's womb, CRM began to breathe and have a heartbeat. The birth date was set. CRM would utter its first sound during the first week of March at Daytona Bike Week. It would be a small sound, unlike most births, but the first words would be, "Jesus loves bikers too."

In addition to attending Florida Christian College in January and February, we had much more that we had to do. In between classes and studying, we continued to repair and renovate both the inside and outside of our bus, while we lived in it. That was also when the first trials began. DQ had to have surgery. Three weeks later, his aunt died. We went to North Carolina for the funeral to be with his mother, and we had no sooner returned to Florida when his grandmother died. We found ourselves back in North Carolina twice in three weeks. The devil knew we wanted to be at Daytona soon, and he tried his best to keep us from it. But alas, too many people were in prayer against him.

The leadership of our home church and of Florida Christian College encouraged us to find a church to serve while we attended college. We wouldn't be content simply attending, we wanted to begin ministering to others. We made some appointments with churches near the college, and were told a few times, "Our church is just not ready for this." One appointment was with the minister of a church in Orlando. He listened to the vision for CRM and invited us back on Sunday. We felt some acceptance at the church, but not to the extent we had hoped. We needed to grow and be challenged. They had no place for us, and we had never been Sunday-only kind of Christians, so we moved on.

On Monday, we had an appointment at the First Christian Church of Orlando with a minister named Joe Cooper. For over an hour, we sat in his office telling him about ourselves and our vision. Joe sat in his chair and listened intently. When we finished, he asked us a few questions and then called in Alan Tison, the youth minister. They offered us the opportunity to teach their kindergarten class (oh, my!). First Christian Church of Orlando wanted and needed us. The congregation welcomed us on Wednesday night. We knew we had found the place God intended for us to be. On Sunday evening, we placed our student membership at *First Church*. We became part of the fellowship that would bless us, help sustain us, and love us while we were at college and away from our home church in Bayonet Point.

All too quickly, the time came for us to depart. We had worked hard, studied hard, and worshipped hard. It was time to put our vision into action. We felt a sense of excitement that we had never experienced before. We also felt an equal sense of fear. We tried hard not to show the fear, but we probably didn't cover it up as well as we thought. First Church sent us off with much love. They gave us an offering that allowed us to pay the bus repairs and begin our trip debt free. The Sunday before we left, Pastor Joe had us stand as he told us how much the congregation had given for us. Had the pew not been in front of us, I believe both DQ and I would have fallen on the floor. We spent the rest of the service with tears of joy streaming down our faces. We had searched for love and brotherhood in the world for many years to no avail. We found real love and acceptance only through Jesus Christ and His people. We had been given an overwhelming sense of love, without condition or measure. Truly, God provides that love through His people, for we humans don't have the capacity to love like that without Him.

On Wednesday night, we attended First Church for the last time before our journey. I had trouble concentrating. As I looked around the room, my excitement for the future diminished. My heart was heavy because of all the friends we would leave behind, even though I had tried not to become attached. The walls that had so often protected me in the past failed me this time. The people's love and warmth had broken through my barriers. I looked at a few of the older saints and wondered if I would see them again this side of heaven. Tears welled up in my eyes. I gazed across the room at some of the other couples and wondered if our friendship would endure the challenges of time and distance that lay ahead.

I thought of the many Sundays and Wednesdays to come when we would enter a strange church for the first time. Would the people who attended those churches love us as our friends do here, or would they see DQ's long hair and my nose ring and walk away? Part of me wanted to scream, "I love you and this is all a mistake! I want to stay here in the fold!" My spirit knew better. The next day, we would embark upon the greatest adventure of our lives and the purpose for which God had created us. My flesh wanted to stay where it was safe, but in my soul, I knew it was time to go.

At the end of the service, we stood up but got no further. Our brothers and sisters in Christ gathered around us and flooded us with warm wishes, gifts, and love. One brother had written a poem for us. We both cried as it was read aloud. This was not "Good-bye," but only "So long." We would all meet again – either here, there, or in the air.

Easy Rider

God loves you, Easy Rider,
Let Him guide you through the night.
Chase the wind, Easy Rider,
Let Him lead you to the Light.

Sometimes, that road goes on and on
And seems to never end;
But keep your eyes wide open,
So you'll meet your next friend.

Your friend may not know Jesus,
'Cause he's living deep in sin.
Tell him about our Lord and Savior,
'Cause it's the only way he'll win.

That old boneshaker rolls on and on
To places far and wide.
You're not alone on your ol' Harley,
'Cause God is by your side.

From the peaks of Carolina
To the plains of the old, old west,
Keep your head up, Easy Rider,
And let God do all the rest.

Livin' on the road is not easy;
  There'll be days of bitter grief.
The rain and heat will come down hard.
  There'll be days with no relief.

There's a song about the bikers –
  You may have heard it once before.
It's from the Fairport Convention,
  Way back in '64:

"Come all ye roving minstrels,
  And together we will try
To raise the spirit of the earth,
  And move the rolling sky."

BMWs, Triumphs, and old Harleys
  Are the symbols of the road;
Leather, chrome, and tattoos
  All worth their weight in gold.

But think about this my fellow biker,
  As my story comes to an end:
God loves you, Easy Rider.
  He wants to be your friend.

So as you go into the night
  From one rally to another,
Remember what Jesus told you:
  To always love your brother.

Go, tell it on the mountain,
  Over the hills and everywhere.
God loves you, Easy Rider.
  We'll keep you in our prayers.

> — John Thompson,
> Orlando, Florida,
> February 26, 1992

Chapter 3

Return to the Foreign Field

The people to whom I am sending you are obstinate and stubborn. Say to them, "This is what the Sovereign LORD says." And whether they listen or fail to listen – for they are a rebellious house – they will know that a prophet has been among them. And you, son of man, do not be afraid of them or their words. Do not be afraid, though briers and thorns are all around you and you live among scorpions. Do not be afraid of what they say or terrified by them, though they are a rebellious house. You must speak my words to them, whether they listen or fail to listen, for they are rebellious. But you, son of man, listen to what I say to you. Do not rebel like that rebellious house. (Ezekiel 2:4-8 NIV)

I am sending you out like sheep among wolves. (Matthew 10:16 NIV)

It was almost Daytona Bike Week. We sat inside the bus eating dinner on TV trays. DQ sat in the recliner, and I used the lid of the porta potty, because those were the only two seats we had. We picked at our food in silence, occasionally looking out the windows. We had physically returned to a place from which we were now emotionally far removed. Both of us feared that time and place. We stayed at the same campground only a few short years earlier. Together we had partied with the best of them, drinking and doing drugs until the money ran out or the week was over – whichever came first. Usually, it was the former.

Now the campground was empty, we were the first to arrive. The next day, others would start to come. They would come on bikes or in cars or vans. They would bring their children, their food, and their alcohol and drugs. Though we didn't speak, DQ and I knew that the questions on our minds were the same: *Would we be tempted to partake? Have we somehow misunderstood this calling? Have we put ourselves in a position to fall?*

We knew many people would be disappointed if we stumbled: our home church at Bayonet Point, that had the faith and vision to ordain us and send us forth; our student church in Orlando, that sent us off with their love and blessings; the staff of Florida Christian College, who ignored their own rules in order to help educate us; and the students there, who encouraged us. The tension in the bus was thick. Would the bikers accept us, or beat us up and burn the tent? Both were very real possibilities.

The 12 x 12' church tent was set up outside. All we could do was wait and see what happened. We prayed but found it impossible to let go of our apprehension, so we prayed some more. Satan screamed in our ears that we should run and leave while we could. He didn't know that we had already passed the point of being able to leave. We had committed to this and would be here until it was over, or they threw us out. DQ and I were both pretty hard-headed about challenges and keeping our word. For the first time in ten years, God was represented at that campground. We begged Him for strength and acknowledged our inability to do the work on our own. He was with us that night, and He would be with us the next.

DQ woke early, with his nerves frayed. I attempted to remain calm and composed for him. It was the Lord's Day, and I encouraged DQ as he went over his sermon again and again. The devil whispered to us that we weren't really ready. In hindsight, we weren't. But how could we be? God would use the events themselves to train us; it was always the school of hard knocks for us.

We combated the evil one with prayer. As DQ practiced, I set up the tent with Bibles and song sheets. The boom box would play prerecorded hymns. We were ready at eleven, but the service wasn't until noon. We paced. Our biggest fear was that no one would come. We prayed and prayed again. It was now eleven fifteen. Our biggest fear now was that someone *would* come. Finally, at eleven forty-five, we went toward the tent, hoping to welcome someone. That took all of two minutes. As we approached the tent, a huge man walked up to DQ and asked, "Is that a Christian flag you're flying? And does that say you're having service at noon?" DQ swallowed hard and affirmed that indeed it was, and indeed we were. The man smiled and said, "Great. Let me go get my Bible, and I'll be right back." As he walked off, we praised God that He was merciful to us and that we didn't have to do this alone.

We ended up with two other people there that morning, and the Holy Spirit filled our little tent. DQ delivered his first sermon on "True Brotherhood," and everyone was challenged by the words the Lord had him speak. That morning, some of our fear left. We knew we were doing what God wanted us to do. That morning, Satan lost a little more of his power over us. We still had a long way to go, though neither of us had any idea how far it actually was. God was only beginning a work that would be unstoppable and powerful in all He ordained it to do.

DQ and I made a simple plan for the week. We would exercise and go for a walk in the mornings. After that, we would set out the jewelry DQ had made, hoping to attract people and tell them about the Savior. That was the plan.

When people visited our table, we tried to share the Lord with them. We were gentle and tried to show them Jesus by loving them. Bibles were laid out on the table beside a handwritten sign that read, "Free." A sign, on the bus, behind the table advertised afternoon Bible studies and Sunday services. The Christian flag waved from the top of the bus, and the church tent stood beside our vending table. On the outside peaks of the tent was a cross made with duct tape. At noon each day, we covered the jewelry table with a blanket and went to the tent to hold Bible studies.

Each day, we prayed for someone to come. Each day, we entered the tent alone. Even though no one came, we remained faithful and hoped that our actions would witness to the people who watched us. We heard a lot of smart remarks, but no one seemed intent on hurting us. We often felt like a sideshow at a circus, but when we felt our lowest, God would send someone our way to encourage us. The big man who came to church that first Sunday was named Mike. We found out that he was a new Christian and was fearful of falling back into his old ways. He had come to help his friend operate a paint booth where pictures were painted on bikes and shirts. That was the first bike event he had been to since his conversion, and he was being greatly tempted. Each time the temptation grew strong, he came over and talked to DQ. Mike told us that our strength helped him from falling back. We knew that if Mike was the only one we helped that week, it was worth everything we had done. We thanked God for Mike.

Members of a production company who wanted to film biker women in action contacted us early in the week. I was cautious, because the image they might try to convey could be inconsistent with what we were trying to do. After the interview,

I felt comfortable with the production company filming our
ladies' Bible study. We set it up for Tuesday afternoon. I awoke
calm, but as the afternoon drew closer, I became increasingly
nervous since no one had attended any of our Bible studies so
far. I was praying hard that the Lord would send someone to
the Bible study. I tried to tell myself that God would take care
of it, but the thought of no one showing up terrified me.

The production team showed up around noon and inter-
viewed me in the bus. When we emerged, there were two women
waiting for the Bible study. Silently, I praised God. Both women
knew that the filming would happen that day. Maybe that is
why they came, but I didn't care. I had a captive audience, and
my first priority was to take the gospel to them. I ignored the
cameras and went for it. About twenty minutes into the Bible
study, DQ stuck his head in the tent and said that the film crew
wanted to finish the interview. I looked at both women and
then back at DQ and boldly proclaimed, "They will have to wait
until we are through. I may never have a chance to share with
these women again, and I'm not cutting it short." DQ smiled
and went away to tell the film crew that I was about God's
business. Neither woman was ready to make a commitment,
but I thanked them for allowing me to share with them, and I
thanked God for allowing them to hear His Word. I had been
true to my calling even if the interview ended up on the cutting room floor. God used the vanity of two women to bring
them to hear the gospel.

One morning, we found a man sleeping in the church tent.
Since it was six in the morning, we didn't wake him. Immediately,
Matthew 25:35 came to our minds: *For I was hungry and you gave
me something to eat, I was thirsty and you gave me something to
drink, I was a stranger and you invited me in* (NIV). The man,
whose name was Tony, finally began to stir at around nine, and
DQ took him a cup of coffee. When DQ entered the tent, Tony

apologized for not asking us if he could sleep there. He said security had told him, "That's the Christians' tent. They won't care." DQ assured him it was fine. The man said it was the best night's sleep he ever had. DQ told him that was because it was God's tent. The two men talked for a long time. Tony told DQ that his mother was a Christian and always prayed for him, but that he hadn't talked to her in three years. DQ assured Tony that the Lord had brought him to us because of his mother's prayers. As Tony walked away, he said he was going to call her. We prayed that God would be merciful to him and continue to draw Tony to Himself.

Daytona Bike Week was over, and we had not fallen. We passed the test, and Christian Riders Ministry would continue. Looking back on it, we realized that it was not quite as scary as we thought it would be. Many things happened that first week in Daytona. Hundreds of people, including many old friends we used to party with, came by to see if we were really doing what everyone said we were doing. Their reaction to us ranged from cordial to hostile. DQ, with tears, begged one friend to change his life. He was so close, but instead got mad and said, "If you were anyone else, DQ, I would punch your lights out." Then he sped away on his Harley, almost killing himself before a watching campground.

It was a hard week, and our resolve to be what God wanted us to be had been tested. There were moments when I wished I could disappear. Other times, I felt as if we were on display. Still other times, I saw glimpses in DQ of what God was doing in us. We had expected to feel as if we had come back and belonged, but we didn't belong to the world anymore. We felt different from the people around us. We didn't feel better than them, by any means, just removed. God had changed us from the inside. We looked as if we belonged, but our looks were deceiving. We were no longer on the inside looking out, but were on the outside looking in, trying to tell others how they could get out. We demonstrated that it was possible to be both Christians and bikers. We knew that we were aliens, and our lives were never again to be our own.

Chapter 4

On the High Wire

Up on the high wire, I hear the crowd begin to call.
Some want you to fly, some want to see you fall.
Now and then I stumble, but I ain't fallen yet.
Your love helps me forget, I'm working without a net.

— Waylon Jennings, "Working Without a Net"

The day finally arrived. We were on our own. Up until that point, we had been secure in the fact that we weren't far from people who loved us. That feeling of security was now gone, left behind as the miles rolled on. We spent our first night in a rest area outside Tallahassee, Florida. Neither of us slept much. Between the truck noise and the exhaust fumes, we could only catnap. I felt alone and quite dependent upon God. I knew we had passed the point of no return. There was nowhere to go but forward, wherever the Lord would lead us. There was a certain amount of excitement in the adventure, but also loneliness. It was DQ, our dog Sporty, and me against the world. Of course, God was with us. But somehow, that fact didn't totally take the edge off the journey.

We knew God was leading us, but we didn't know where

or why. Being quite new to that life, we just knew to follow our instincts and stay in prayer. The third day of our travels, we ended up at a truck stop just outside Charlotte, North Carolina. We tried to find a rest area, but none allowed overnight parking. The truck stop had a dirt parking lot, so we had to keep the windows closed due to the dust. After a quick dinner of canned beans, we went to bed. We left the radio playing to drown out some of the noise from the semi-trucks' engines. I awoke at two in the morning to find DQ watching me sleep. He told me he had just heard a commercial on the radio about the Charlotte Swap Meet. The "motorcycle flea market" was scheduled for that same morning. We prayed together and decided that God had led us there for that. If we would have stayed at the rest area, we wouldn't have been able to pick up the Charlotte radio station. We got up and drove to the fairgrounds. We were the first vendors in line when they opened the gate at eleven.

Rick, the man in charge of the gate, was an old friend of DQ's. Rick was pleased to see us again. He asked DQ if he wanted to be right next to the stage. That was a prime location and the center of activities, but DQ thanked him but told him no. It was also where the wet T-shirt contests and other craziness went on. We didn't need or want to be right next to that the whole time. Instead, Rick gave us a booth in one of the other buildings. He told us we could park next to the building and sleep there in our bus. We had our booth set up by about three o'clock that afternoon. Tommy and Shirley, the people in the booth behind us, were also Christians. They were new Christians, and we were able to greatly encourage them. A group of white supremacists set up right across from us. We laughed, knowing God has a wonderful sense of humor. They were selling hate, and we were giving away love. What an irony. We prayed that God's love would prevail.

Many people came by the booth to look at the jewelry, but it was difficult to witness to them. When we turned the conversation to spiritual things, they looked at us as if we were crazy, and then they walked away. Once, while DQ was away getting coffee, a group of "clubbers" came by. The men in the group harassed me. It unnerved me, but I refused to show it. The women who were with them seemed embarrassed by the comments made to me. I prayed that my witness would stick in those women's minds as seeds planted that only God could water.

One fellow who had watched us all day finally summoned the courage to come over and talk. He waited until DQ left, and then he asked me with all seriousness, "Do you really believe in Jesus?" I assured him that I did with all my heart. He went on to say that each time he had tried to seek Jesus, people put him down for the way he looked, with his long hair and tattoos. I shared a tract with him. It described how the religious leaders of Jesus' day treated Him and how Jesus' friends were social rejects. I encouraged him not to give up. He took a Bible, but wasn't ready to give his life to Jesus. More seeds planted. As he walked away, tears filled my eyes. How many people reject Jesus because of self-righteous Christians? How many people will burn in hell because of someone's attitude of superiority? May God have mercy on that "Christian's" soul on judgment day. I bowed my head and prayed for him and others like him. I prayed for our world full of social rejects, for all the people whom no one loves, and for the strength and wisdom to lead some of those tormented souls to the King.

The Charlotte Swap Meet ended Sunday evening around six o'clock. We had sold enough jewelry to pay for our admission, and we thanked God for His provision. By the time we packed up, it was late and we were hungry. We hadn't eaten much all weekend. It was hard to be vegetarians at those events. I hadn't had time to prepare food during the busy weekend, and most of what the venders sold was junk food. We stayed in the parking lot for the night. It was quiet, free, and I could fix us a good dinner. We left exhausted, both physically and spiritually. It had been hard holding ourselves in check all weekend, being so careful of every word we said and of everywhere we looked. It had been a good weekend, though. And while we were glad we had come, we were glad to be done. We felt that God had used us some, but that He had trained us more. We knew not where He was taking us, but we were willing to go the distance no matter the cost.

Chapter 5

Many Trials

Consider it pure joy, my brothers, whenever you
face trials of many kinds, because you know that
the testing of your faith develops perseverance.
Perseverance must finish its work so that you may
be mature and complete, not lacking anything.
(James 1:2-4 NIV)

While we were in North Carolina, we visited DQ's family for three weeks before going on the extended part of our journey. God had given us a vision. Once we left North Carolina, we knew we would follow God's calling for us to set up a church tent at the Buffalo Chip Campground during the Sturgis Motorcycle Rally in South Dakota. We had never been to that campground, but we knew it was one of the largest in Sturgis. It was also known as "The Best Party Anywhere."

Our first week in North Carolina was nice. We saw a lot of our old friends and told them about our lives and plans. They were amazed at the change in us. We tried to witness to them and let them see the light that was now in our lives. Many of them were hard-hearted, but they still loved us. As long as that love remained, we felt we had a chance to show them Jesus.

On Wednesday, though, the difficulties began. We headed to the next town over to get a crown of thorns tattooed on each of our right wrists. We had been in prayer about it for months and felt it was the right thing to do. Our witness with the bikers would be strengthened, especially the hardcore ones. They believe if something means life or death to you, you tattoo it on your body. When we would extend our right hands to them, they would have no doubt that Jesus meant everything to us.

We got on DQ's Harley Shovel/Pan and left. It was a gorgeous day, and we were praising God for His impact in our lives. We were running about sixty miles per hour, when the kicker plate in the transmission locked. The kick pedal on the outside spun backwards with the force and speed of the engine. It knocked DQ's foot forward, and then hit the toes of my boot. DQ looked down to see the pedal spinning around as he pulled off the highway. He asked me if I was all right, but I didn't know. There was a dent in my boot, and my foot felt like it was on fire. I couldn't tell if it was broken, bleeding, or just slightly injured. I sat down, and he helped me unlace my boot. We praised God that my foot was only bruised. DQ looked at me and said, "I guess Satan doesn't want us to get them tattoos."

We quickly attempted to push-start the bike. Since it had no electric start, it was our only option. On the third try, it fired to life. I praised God, because I thought I was about to have a heart attack pushing the bike down the road. DQ circled back around for me. We laughed as we roared away. Satan wasn't going to stop these children of God from wearing the mark of our Lord. Two hours later, we each had a beautiful crown of thorns around our wrist. We prayed that they would always glorify God. We had a friend come pick us up and take us home, fearing that the Harley might get damaged if we rode it any more. Tim, our mechanic buddy, came over and told us that it would take about $250 to fix it. We told him to go ahead and fix it, since we had to have it. God would provide the money; we trusted Him.

The next day, Thursday, we rode my Triumph motorcycle since DQ's was getting fixed. A friend had just rebuilt the top end of my motor, so we felt pretty safe. We were on a mission to reconcile with a long-time friend whom we had alienated before we came to the Lord. We had a wonderful visit. God healed hearts and allowed us to share our newfound faith.

We left, but hadn't gone too far when we heard a roar from the bottom of the motor. We rode to the Triumph mechanic's home. The mechanic examined the bike and informed us that the bottom end needed attention. He said it would cost about $400 and take him three weeks to fix. We called around to see if we could find another bottom end. The couple we had met in Charlotte happened to have one, so on Friday we went and got it. Having that bottom end would speed repair time from three weeks to one and also cut the cost by more than half. We had to have the motorcycle repaired, because we needed it for transportation. We praised God for allowing all that to happen before we went out west, where we didn't know anyone. Money would be real tight, but God had foreseen everything and had already provided for us.

With everything breaking, we had the bus engine checked out before we left. DQ's cousin, Danny, came over on Saturday and examined the bus. After listening to it for twenty minutes, Danny came in the house and told me to sit. I hate when that happens. Who says that when they have good news? "There's no easy way to say it," he said. "The motor is trashed. It will need a new crank, lifters, and maybe a cam. There is no way to tell the extent till we tear into it." The saving news was that Danny could do the work and had room for the bus in his yard. We went to Danny's place in Durham on Tuesday so the repairs could begin. We felt like we couldn't catch a break.

A couple from our home church in Bayonet Point had volunteered to send us our mail every week. Our mail packet arrived shortly after Danny left. We anxiously opened the package, starving for words from home. Instead, we found a letter from the IRS informing us that we owed them $595. We laid the letter aside and said aloud, "Lord, we need $595 to pay this."

I sorted through a few more pieces of mail, and then opened a letter that contained a check for our house insurance refund. It was $614. God is so very good. We looked at each other and said, "The Lord gives and the tax man takes away. Blessed be the Lord."

We had many problems that week, but God systematically took care of each one. We were sure that God was fixing things now, so the rest of the trip would be easier. It was a nice thought, but proved to be untrue. The truth was that the closer we got to Sturgis, the harder the powers of darkness would attempt to break us down and send us scurrying home with our heads hung low in defeat. God would use the time until Sturgis to unite us as never before, raising us up to where He needed us to be, fully dependent upon Him.

Chapter 6

Easter Morning

For since the creation of the world God's invisible qualities – his eternal power and divine nature – have been clearly seen, being understood from what has been made, so that men are without excuse. (Romans 1:20 NIV)

The alarm went off at 4:30 a.m., and we groaned as we rolled out of bed. We wanted that Easter morning to be special. It would be the first of many Easters we would spend in the service of the Lord. My stomach growled loudly. We hadn't eaten for four days, but instead had spent that time in prayer and communion with our Master. We dressed quickly, and DQ fired up his Harley for a sunrise putt to the lake. With my Bible under my arm, I seated myself on the pillow that was bungeed to his luggage rack. We roared off into the damp, dark morning. In the darkness, the dogwood blooms in the forest looked like newly fallen snow. My mind drifted to my Savior, my risen Savior. What a glorious day that first Easter morning was when Jesus defeated death and Satan. I sang and prayed and worshipped God during the hour ride.

We pulled off the road at the side of the lake and read the account of the resurrection of Jesus Christ from all four gospels. We both felt very close to God as we looked over the lake and watched the sun rise above the water. Everything seemed brighter and more alive. The lack of food had heightened our senses. We could smell the water and even seemed to smell the trees for the first time. We watched in amazement as the dew glistened off a spider web. A hawk above us lifted his voice to worship the Creator. For a few minutes, everything seemed to slow down, and only what we saw and felt in our souls seemed real. We sat in silence, wishing it would never end. Then we broke into song and, with the hawk, lifted our feeble voices to heaven.

Chapter 7

You're My One Thing

Every night and every day
You hold on tight
Or you drift away,
And you're left to live

With the choices you make.
Oh, Lord please give me the strength
To watch and work and love and sing and pray.
. . . You're my one thing!
— Rich Mullins, "My One Thing"

The front of the bus was dismantled and sitting in Danny's driveway, looking like it should go to the junkyard. The entire grill and one fender had been removed, along with half the engine. It wasn't as bad as they expected. We *only* needed a cam, lifters, clutch, a throw-out bearing, and a pressure plate. It would cost about $400. We were totally tapped out and relying on God.

We had hoped that the bus would be repaired in time for the Cherokee Spring Swap Meet, but as the days went by, it became obvious that there was no chance of that happening. The parts wouldn't be in until the Monday after the event, and Danny and DQ would still have to put it all back together. The swap meet was that weekend. DQ and I talked about it and decided we had no option but to cancel. We called the people who rented the vendor spaces and let them know that we were going to have to cancel. They curtly informed us that we wouldn't get our money back. I hadn't expected it back.

When DQ explained to Danny that we were canceling the weekend event, because we had no way to travel the 200 miles to get there, Danny said, "You're not canceling. You can take my new pickup truck." DQ and I looked at each other and said, "Cool. That will work." We realized then that although we had talked to each other about our problem, we had forgotten to talk to God about it. That was our mistake. We saw that God was making a way, through Danny, for us to go, and go we would.

The alarm went off on Thursday at 7:00 a.m., and we rolled out of bed and got to work. Danny put a full-size mattress in the back of the pickup, and it took up the entire bed of the truck. The truck was very full by the time we finished loading it. We were thankful, though, that we were able to go minister. We left our little furry child, Sporty, with Danny, and we drove up to the mountains with joyful hearts, wondering what God had in store for us. By that evening, we were checked into a campground and had the tent set up at the Ceremonial Grounds. The show started in the morning at ten. I sure missed my Sporty to cuddle with.

What a wonderful day it was. We were able to share our faith with many people, and DQ even gave a Bible away. We met some folks who were with two different Christian motorcycle groups. They seemed like nice folks, but not much like us. It's hard to describe. They seemed to be business-like people who also rode motorcycles. They were clean-cut and proper, which is all right. God has folks for all of us to minister to.

Saturday was quite different than Friday. The temperature dropped to just above freezing. We sold our jewelry and talked to people. Many folks seemed interested in the jewelry until we started getting on spiritual ground. Then, just like at the Charlotte Swap Meet, they quickly left. Oh well. We were there to talk about the change Jesus had made in our lives, and not to make money. We attended another group's morning church services. We got really convicted by the Lord that we should be doing a service ourselves. We were willing.

Sunday morning dawned cold and snowing. We hadn't packed long johns or leather pants, and I couldn't stand another day of freezing. I sat in the booth, shaking from the cold. Many of the vendors were leaving. We went to our booth and prayed about it, and God gave us a peace about heading out. We loaded up the truck and headed back to Durham. The mountains were beautiful with a light white dusting over everything, but the roads got bad quickly, confirming that we had made the right decision. We felt light-hearted and knew we had done the Lord's will that weekend. We had put Him first, before our comfort or convenience. No matter what, we would be faithful and knew God was our *one thing*.

Chapter 8

The Lady Can Ride

My hands were shaking like a drunk who had been without a drink for far too long. The butterflies in my stomach assured me that was not my problem. I needed to get my motorcycle endorsement for the first time, so I could ride legally. My automobile driver's license, that I had since I was fifteen years old, didn't count. Up until then, I had only ridden off-road. I passed the written test for my motorcycle endorsement two weeks earlier. That was a piece of cake. I had no fear of written tests, but this was different. I would have to perform a skills test to see if I was worthy and able to ride my motorcycle on the street. At that moment, I was sure that I wasn't worthy, and there was a chance I wasn't even able to do so. To top off the stress, we were leaving for Gulfport, Mississippi, as soon as I passed. That meant no second chance. I either flew or fell. I would, in all probability, be all right if I could keep from throwing up during the test.

We unloaded my 1965 Triumph Bonneville from the trailer and kick-started her to life. We didn't want her to stop running, because we knew that she might not start again in the cold weather. The carburetors weren't synchronized correctly, but as long as I kept giving the gas a gentle twist, she stayed running. I had practiced so much for this.

DQ was not an easy teacher. I understood that he didn't want to be responsible for me killing myself. He had taken me to a church parking lot to learn. First, he had me start and stop to get used to the clutch. We did this over and over and over again. Convinced that I had mastered the clutch, he let me start circling cones until I was dizzy and bored to death. I may not have been ready for the street, but I could circle cones really well, in a figure eight or any other way. After what seemed like endless days of cone-circling, DQ finally let me take my Triumph to a huge vacant parking lot and shift gears. I went up to third, back down to first, and then to a complete stop. DQ looked at me and said, "Again." When I couldn't take it anymore, I said, "I am ready." To this he smugly replied, "You'll be ready when I say you're ready." So, off I went, again and again.

I wished that I was back in that parking lot, but DQ said I was now ready. As we waited for the examiner to come, I struck up a conversation with a fellow rider who was also there to take the test. He seemed very confident.

"How long have you been riding on the street?" he asked me.

"I haven't ridden on the street yet, because I have no endorsement."

He looked shocked and replied, "I've been riding illegally for six months, so I could get enough experience to pass this test. This is my second try."

At that moment, I started praying. Truly, only God could get me through this. Only He could make it happen that day.

The examiner arrived and graciously said, "Ladies first. I know the manual says that you have to perform two of the four exercises listed, but my state supervisor is here, and I need you to perform all four exercises – and I'm going to add one more."

I wondered if she was allowed to do that, but then I reminded myself that she had a badge and could probably do anything she wanted. *Why me? Why today?* She held the future of my riding experience in her hands, so I remained quiet. Oh, well. Let's go for it. DQ stood across the street praying for me, and I hoped he was praying hard.

The first thing the examiner told me to do was to stall the motorcycle and restart it as quickly as possible. I looked at her as if she was nuts. I had practiced keeping that old thing running, not stalling it out. I had no idea how to make it stall. Without thinking, I held on tightly and dumped the clutch. The old girl lurched violently forward and the engine stopped. As I quickly jumped up on the seat to kick-start her (there was no electric start on the bike), I prayed, "Please God, let her start on the first kick." With the first down sweep of my leg, she roared back to life. I silently prayed, "Thank you, Jesus."

The next four tests were basic. The examiner gave me clear instructions on each one: "Go straight forward, shift to second, give a right turn signal, downshift to first, and turn left at the cone." I did it all except the turn signal. After three more sets of instructions, the examiner decided that I was an expert at the cones. Thank you, DQ. At the end, she smiled, signed the paper, and said, "Good job. You only lost one point. Go get your picture made." It was the goofiest picture ever made. I didn't know a person could smile that largely. It was surpassed only by the look of pride on DQ's smiling face. As I exited the building, I held up my license and screamed, "This thing here says I'm a biker. Look out world, the lady can ride!"

Chapter 9

Scattered Friends

*A man of many companions may come to ruin, but
there is a friend who sticks closer than a brother.*
(Proverbs 18:24 ESV)

We headed south from North Carolina. The extra money we began with was gone, so from that point on, we had to live on DQ's monthly pension for everything – both ministry and personal needs. The bus ended up eating about $1,000, but we got a rebuilt engine and new brakes all around. The bikes used up another $1,000, but they seemed to be running well after the repairs. That gave both of us transportation when the school bus was parked. A multitude of emotions filled my heart: fear, excitement, apprehension, and wonder. Through it all, only the positive feelings ruled my heart. I knew God was in control of all of it, and He would take us where He needed us to be.

Since we had four days until we were supposed to be at the Gulfport drag races, we stopped in Pensacola to see some friends. They didn't know about the great change God had made in us, so we knew it would be an interesting weekend. After we arrived at their house, we learned that they were moving the next day. We laughed and figured that God had sent us to help. We spent the weekend in wonderful fellowship and sharing. Too soon, it was time to leave, but we were able to give them Bibles before we departed.

On our way out of town, we drove past a biker bar. When the bikers saw the old, brown school bus pulling a trailer with two motorcycles, the group yelled and motioned for us to come join their party. We smiled and DQ proclaimed, "Aren't they going to be surprised at what they get?" We ended up spending the afternoon at the bar, playing pool, drinking sodas, and talking to people. God blessed me with the opportunity to pray with a man named Dale. He once walked with God, but had since traveled far down the wrong road. He never realized that it was possible to be both a Christian and a biker. "It is a long road away from God, but just one small step back," was my encouragement to Dale before we departed. What an awesome thing to be led by God in every detail of life, such as when to wake up, which road to take, and where to stop every night.

We headed out of town and hoped to make it to Gulfport, Mississippi, that night. God had other plans. At the edge of town, we stopped at Hardee's for a milkshake to cool us down on that hot, Gulf Coast afternoon. As I stepped out of the bus, I heard a hiss coming from the front tire. I smiled at DQ and told him of the latest development. He sighed and pulled the bus around back, out of the traffic pattern. As we sipped our milkshakes, I went to the payphone to call our emergency roadside service. The operator put me on hold for a little while, and then informed me that no one would change our tire. It seemed that the split rims on the old bus were dangerous and could possibly decapitate people. She did have a dealer on the other line, though, who said that he would come out and fix us up with the new rims for $160 each.

I thanked her and then went to talk to DQ. We didn't have

the money for one rim, let alone four. DQ told me to call the operator back and have her call the tire dealer who fixed our rear tire earlier in the week. The operator called the dealer, who said, "I know who they are. Tell them I'll be there in forty-five minutes." I thanked the lady and thanked God for His gracious provision. Then, fear crept into my heart. I wasn't used to being so short of money. Always before, we could at least budget. We had experienced so many unexpected expenses in such a short amount of time that it was staggering.

We drank our milkshakes and waited for Carl, the tire dealer, to appear. It took him the better part of an hour, but finally we saw his service truck. We watched as Carl stepped out and then went around and opened the door on the passenger side of the truck. Out emerged a teenage girl who looked less than thrilled to be there, but she remained polite and quiet. Carl introduced his daughter, Nicole, to us and said, "She really needs to hear about who you are and what you do."

While Carl fixed the tire, we talked and shared our story with Nicole. Even after the tire was fixed, we all sat on the curb and continued to talk. We tried to encourage Nicole without coming down on her or telling her what to do. She remained quiet, but listened intently to all we said. So often, young people just need to see that they have choices in life. They are never without options regarding the choices that lay before them.

Three hours after Carl and Nicole arrived, they departed. Carl refused to accept any money from us, and we would never see them again. We slept in Pensacola that night, blessed to know that because of a flat tire, we were able to speak to a young lady about God. Because of a breakdown, Jesus had been exalted. And despite tough times, we had been faithful in following the Holy Spirit's leading. A soul was spared, and a life had been changed for Jesus Christ. What a day!

Chapter 10

The Road Less Traveled

I shall be telling this with a sigh,
Somewhere ages and ages hence:
Two roads diverged in a wood, and I –
I took the one less traveled by,
And that has made all the difference.
— Robert Frost, "The Road Not Taken"

While traveling down the road, I pulled out my journal and wrote:

"As a child, I discovered Robert Frost. My dear grandmother opened my young mind to the poet. At such a young age, I couldn't understand the vast majority of his work, but I found a connection with many of his poems. Robert Frost inspired me to write, create, and catalog my own thoughts, dreams, and difficulties. I wrote my first poem at the age of five, and while my poem was juvenile in nature, it held a sort of passion not seen in most children's writings.

"Of all of Frost's writings, "The Road Not Taken" was my favorite. To me, it was about more than a minor decision in the woods. It was about life and the choice of a lifetime. Even as a child, I knew God had a mission for me, and it would be on a road "less traveled." At the age of eight, I felt the call to be a missionary. Somehow, during my teenage years, I lost sight of that call.

"Now, bouncing down the roads of America in a school bus, the words of Mr. Frost echo in my mind: 'Two roads diverged in a wood, and I – I took the one less traveled by, and that has made all the difference.'"

My journal continued:

> *"Gone now are our family and friends. We are separated from all things familiar and comfortable. The only thing we have for the next seven months is God and each other. I look over at DQ and wonder if I even know him. In a sense, I don't know him any more than he knows me. We are such different people than we were even a mere year ago. It seems as if everything is turned upside down. Yet, in a strange and profound sense, it has been righted in doing so. Everything is perfectly logical now, while our past is wildly bizarre. While the road and the loneliness are foreign, it is here that God needs us to be, to teach us dependence on Him and on each other.*

> *"I think about what I hope to accomplish this year. My strongest desire is to see other people, people like me, come to know Jesus. I don't want to introduce them to Jesus in the religious way that American culture had made my God to be. The picture of a white-skinned, long-haired, blue-eyed Jesus with delicate features is strange to me. This Jesus has little meaning to the people for which my heart aches. I want them to meet the real Jesus – the Jesus who 2,000 years ago, laid down His life for the*

dysfunctional DQs and Beths of this gnarly world. The Jesus I know was Jewish to the bone and broke every man-made tradition that the religious leaders of His day held sacred. I want them to see the Jesus who has saved my life, marriage, and sanity. That Jesus will matter to these hard-headed scooter people. God has called us to this, and though I feel inadequately prepared, He must have a plan in mind. As God of the universe, He has to, because we surely didn't think this mission up on our own!"

Chapter 11

Rebels Without a Clue

It was a very hot and sultry Thursday, but not even the heat or the fact that we had to wait in line for three-and-a-half hours could dampen our excitement. We had made it to Biloxi, Mississippi, for the Gulfport Drags. The people running the event let us in as Christian jewelers and allowed us to erect the church tent. The lady who registered us was a Christian. No doubt God had placed her there to assist us. We had all day to set up the church tent and a small tarp to shade us where we sold the jewelry. The general public wouldn't be allowed in until the next day. Our excitement mounted as we waited to see what God had in store for us that weekend.

The people rolled in on Saturday, and the drag strip fired up too. There was a steady stream of people who looked at the jewelry, but as usual, when we interjected Jesus they quickly left. By late afternoon, we were discouraged. We were also discouraged by the nudity that was taking place, something we had never seen as prevalent at any other motorcycle rally. As a storm approached, we were thankful for the break. We put things away that could be damaged by the rain and retreated to the bus.

As the rain poured out of the heavens, DQ and I got on our knees and cried out to the Lord, "Why, oh why, Lord, have you sent us out here when no one will listen to us speak your name?" (Woe is us.) When we finally quieted down, the answer came. "If I filled up the tent, you wouldn't know what to say or do, so why should I entrust these people to you?" God was absolutely right, of course. We were like the blind man who only knew that he once was blind but now could see, and that a man named Jesus had healed him.

God had ordained us and called us to minister to those people. How dare we just show up and expect them to fall on their knees, when we hadn't even committed the scriptural plan of salvation to memory. We hadn't prayed for the people in advance. We had a burden, but little else. We decided then and there that we would change. We wrote out a list of Bible verses and began memorizing them immediately. We committed to arrive at future rallies early, so we could pray for those who would come. We might not have been of use to God that day, but by the next event we would do better.

The rain lifted and so did our downcast spirits. The rest of the weekend was an intense spiritual battle. Nakedness, drunkenness, and an evil veil that was hard to pierce prevailed at the event. Yet, we were firm in our commitment, and God led several people our way. We gave out Bibles, and we each led someone to Christ. Another person, who defined his religion as paganism, invited us to his home to talk more. When we left Biloxi, we knew that we had planted some seeds. We also knew that God had changed us, and because of that change, we would be used in the future to affect many others for all eternity. Perhaps our greatest asset at that point was our willingness to submit everything to our Lord and Master.

Chapter 12

A Lesson in Asking

Truly, truly, I say to you, if you ask the Father for anything in My name, He will give it to you. Until now you have asked for nothing in My name; ask and you will receive, so that your joy may be made full. (John 16:23-24 NASB)

We crossed the Texas state line with excitement and discouragement all wrapped up in one package. The excitement was there, because we were in uncharted territory. Neither of us had ever been to Texas before, and we knew God was leading us to Houston. The discouragement was because of more breakdowns; both bikes acted up after Gulfport. DQ's Shovelhead had been running badly, and after being adjusted, it refused to crank at all. We did manage to get the Triumph going after re-jetting the carburetors. We wondered if things would ever get on a smoother level.

On the outskirts of Houston's metropolitan area, we stopped and made a phone call. Before we had left Bayonet Point, Pastors Mel and Mike gave us a highlighted copy of the *Directory of the Ministry*, which listed all the Christian Churches/Churches of Christ across the country. The highlights meant that we could drop Mel or Mike's name. Westside Christian Church in Bellaire, Texas, had been highlighted in orange as Mel's contact. DQ called the minister and casually dropped Mel Gresham's name. After a pause, DQ said, "You do know Mel Gresham, don't you?"

Pastor Harold Eye replied, "Oh yes, I know Mel." Harold invited us to the church and visited with us. After talking with him for a little while, he excused himself. We suspected that he was calling Bayonet Point, and we were right. When he returned, we learned that we had passed the reference check. Harold told us why he had acted so strangely. He was Mel Gresham's brother-in-law. I guess he really did know Mel. We all had a great laugh.

What a wonderful rest we had staying behind the church. It was a rest we didn't even know we needed. It was so quiet compared to the truck stops and rest areas where we had been camping. Even the train that came by every two hours and laid on its air horns a mere 300 yards away seemed like a minor distraction in comparison to the smell of diesel fumes and the constant grinding of gears.

When Harold's wife, Carolyn, asked us if we would consider staying for the week to help with vacation Bible school, we knew, in part, why God had sent us there. We had no idea that our first visit to Texas would begin such a long and joyous relationship with that church. We had been praying for God to use us, and Carolyn had been praying for VBS helpers. The two prayer requests were answered simultaneously, as God sent two wet-behind-the-ears missionaries to teach the children songs about Jesus and to share their passion for the lost. DQ painted a sign advertising VBS for the front yard of the church. We spent a wonderful week with the children and members of that sweet church. On the final day of Bible school, we had a prayer circle. Many of the children prayed for us not to leave. The hardest thing about the life God called us to might be all the leaving. As we pulled out of the church parking lot, people stood in the front yard and lined the street, waving goodbye.

The time spent in Houston had been uplifting and encouraging. Once again, we were on our way to Sturgis, and we knew God had many things in store for us. We had no clue about the severe tests and trails we would have to pass through before we were fit to stand for Jesus Christ at the Buffalo Chip Campground in Sturgis. If we had known, we might have turned back right then.

Chapter 13

Hard Times in Babylon

The wonderful feelings of fun, fellowship, and usefulness were gone. At each junction during the seven weeks after we left Houston, we experienced opposition, rejection, and breakdowns. Though we met some wonderful brothers and sisters in Christ, we were steadily beaten down by everything else. We were about ready to call it quits and go back to Florida with our tails between our legs, beaten and defeated. We almost believed that we had dreamed the whole thing up outside of God's will. It just no longer seemed worth it, and the vision had faded to the background, carried by the tidal wave of opposition.

It all began after we left Houston. We planned to spend our wedding anniversary in Big Bend National Park, camping beside the Rio Grande River. For years, DQ had told me of its beauty, he had seen the Rio Grande from New Mexico. We thought it would also provide a time for us to relax and regroup. I had stated emphatically that I didn't want to spend our wedding anniversary traveling. We arrived at the Rio Grande campground during the sweltering summer heat. The mercury climbed past 111 degrees. Yet, with little humidity, it was tolerable but not comfortable by any means.

Near sunset, we went for a short walk to the river and looked forward to seeing the moon rise and the temperature drop. A hearty breeze had maintained itself all day and promised to usher in a cool night. It wasn't to be. As the mountains swallowed the sun, the wind also took its leave. The temperature never dropped below 95 degrees. DQ smiled and assured me that we were fine. We prepared to spend the evening in the cool of the bus, but our generator refused to cooperate. The motor of our ten-month-old Coleman generator purred along, but it produced no power. So we lay in the stifling heat of the school bus all night in a puddle of sweat.

At six in the morning, we could stand it no longer, so we went outside. DQ suggested packing up and getting out of there before the heat of the day set in. I refused to travel. It was my anniversary. By nine it was 105 degrees. Now *I* suggested to DQ, "Let's pack up and get out of here." We were on the road in fifteen minutes. I had very rarely seen DQ move that fast.

The park ranger assured us that our school bus and open trailer could handle the northern exit road, so we headed north. My Triumph fell over on the trailer, but we retrieved it with no damage done. What the ranger was thinking, we will never know. The 12-15 percent mountain grades were not what DQ wanted to see or what he considered to be an acceptable pull. Our fuel was running out, even though we had filled up in the basin. DQ looked at me and said, "We aren't going to make it out of here!" I laid my hands on the dash of the bus and commenced praying. At one point, DQ shifted from low range second to low range first gear, and the bus went backwards. I prayed harder, earnestly begging God's mercy.

About twenty-five miles from Alpine, in the middle of the desert wilderness, the gas gauge hit *E*. We had no extra fuel on board. Experience had taught us that the bus needed fuel immediately at that point, or she would die. We had no options.

No other vehicles had passed us in the two hours we spent climbing north. DQ and I prayed harder. God looked down on our predicament with mercy, and we rolled into the first gas station in Alpine with the motor still running. It had been on empty for over forty-five minutes. We knew God had been with us, and we had experienced a miracle.

As DQ filled up the old bus, a beautiful motorhome pulled into the gas station. A retired gentleman exited and began to fill the gas tank of his expensive rig. We were longingly gazing at the nice house on wheels when Joe, the motorhome's owner, walked over to us. As he looked over our school bus, he said with a hint of regret, "Wow. You kids have it made. Our first rig was a lot like this. I miss her so. We lived in that bus and made her a part of ourselves, just like you two have done." He admired the curtains and bedspread made of jean material. He looked at DQ and said, "Enjoy that thing." He motioned over his shoulder to his rig as if with contempt and said, "The wife makes me take my shoes off at the door. Imagine that! It sure isn't a home like you have. Enjoy these days, for soon they will be gone." We smiled at the irony of it all. Why is it that we humans are never content with the blessings we have? Too quickly, we would have almost given away what we had. And just as quickly, Joe would have given anything to get it all back.

We continued to drive until we found a campground. Then, we turned the air conditioner on as high as it would go and played Bible trivia in our skivvies until the goose bumps came. Contentment filled our souls as DQ and I thanked God for that place, for the encouragement, but most of all, for our seventh wedding anniversary and our love that was being renewed day by day. Neither of us dwelt on how close we had come to not having any of those blessings, much less each other. For that night, it was enough to gaze at each other and stay wrapped in God's love and approval. We had a happy anniversary with a great story that we could hold onto for years to come.

Chapter 14

Border Crossing

The church in El Paso warmly welcomed us, even though they didn't know us. To save money, we parked at the army base campground on Saturday, but we were required to take a weekend class before we were allowed to ride our motorcycles on the base. The class was only offered every other month, and so was not a possibility for us. We called the church and were given the names and phone number of a couple who might be willing to give us a ride to worship on Sunday. The couple not only took us to church, but kept us all afternoon, feeding us and fellowshipping with us. It was a great day. We were asked to speak that night at church, so we challenged the congregation to look for and seek what God would do through them in their community. Too often, instead of asking God what He wants for us, we do what we want and then ask God to bless it. Our friends at the church told us it was just the message they needed to hear.

Lying in bed, I had a very clear image come to mind. A larger-than-life image of a father and a small child stood before me. All of the little girl's trust and confidence was fully placed in the father, who had the wisdom to lead her and the strength to protect her. I felt as if the Lord had taken my hand and said, "Hold tightly, my dear child, for here we go. Together, we will move mountains." I knew I must hold tightly, for this was truly the journey of a lifetime.

On Monday, DQ and Brent, the El Paso pastor, took the broken generator to Kmart for a repair or replacement. Kmart referred them to a repair center. The repair center refused to do any warranty work for Coleman, stating that the company didn't pay its bills. DQ and Brent were then escorted to the door. DQ prayed as he tried to keep his emotions in check. Then they went back to Kmart. The head manager was called and took the pair to his office. He called Coleman directly. When they refused to do anything, the manager turned to the men and said, "You bought this generator ten months ago from Kmart in Florida in good faith. It has a one-year warranty. I am going to give you a full refund. Then I will contact Coleman and discuss our future business relationship with them in order to get our money back. Thank you, Mr. Roberts, for doing business with Kmart." They left with the full purchase price in hand. We praised God for leading us to a manager who had the integrity to do the right thing. Also, we decided that we might want to shop around for a different brand generator.

With our business behind us, Pastor Brent wanted to take us across the border to Mexico. DQ was hesitant, but Brent assured him that the border towns were very safe. Besides, he knew his way around, and we wanted some hand-painted Mexican tiles to finish the kitchen countertops in the bus. We probably, or rather, definitely, should have listened to DQ.

Getting into Mexico wasn't the difficult part. In fact, it proved to be the easiest part of the day. Shopping wasn't too bad, as my Spanish from college was still pretty good. Even so, we never did locate authentic hand-painted tiles, though we found some cheap, made-in-China imitations. With night approaching, we headed back to El Paso. The line of cars moved slowly across the bridge as the border guards questioned people before allowing them to enter the United States. I guess we looked like a mismatched bunch. Brent looked like a college student, complete with the alligator on his polo shirt. DQ and I looked like bikers. Our biker look couldn't simply be washed off.

The border guard asked each of us our country of citizenship, and we told him that we were from America. He asked us what we had to declare. "Nothing," Brent said. "We were looking for hand-painted tiles but couldn't find any."

I'm sure I saw the hair on the guard's arm stand up. The guard asked if we had bought anything.

"No," came the reply.

"Whose car is this?" the guard questioned.

When Brent spoke, our hearts sank. "Well, it belongs to a friend of mine who is in the service. He's out of the country. I'm not sure where he is right now, but he let me use the car while he's gone. I don't have proof of that, though."

The guard looked ahead at the lanes to the right where the suspicious vehicles were stripped and searched for drugs. There were already cars in each of the search lanes. He began to question us all over again, seeking an independent reply from each of us. "You're citizens of what country?" This went on for fifteen minutes as he waited for a lane to open up. Visions of the inside of a Mexican prison danced through our heads. When no lanes opened up after the sixth round of questioning, the border guard groaned and said, "Get out of my face, NOW!" Brent started to say something, but DQ gave him *the look*.

We all said, "Thank you, sir," and Brent hit the gas. The guard was probably certain he had just let two fugitives and a carload of drugs into the United States. What he really did was ensure that two missionaries never again trusted their freedom to a young preacher without inquiring more about him.

The ladies of the church heard our tile story and took me back a few days later. I was almost kidnapped but averted that experience by running into a crowd. The second store we visited had lovely, hand-painted tiles, and our mission was accomplished. Even so, I made sure to buy a few more things, so it looked to the border guards like we had a good shopping trip.

Chapter 15

Bad Hair Day

From El Paso, Texas, we went to Santa Fe, New Mexico, where the trials continued. We found Santa Fe to be very spiritually repressive and filled with New Age religion. We stayed at a church there, since they had a place on their property for us to hook up. Even though we had the church's address, we had trouble finding it. After driving around for a while, we called the preacher and asked him where the church was. He informed us that the church was actually a skating rink. No wonder we couldn't find it.

It seemed that many of the people in Santa Fe had a very negative image of evangelical Christians. Too many Christians had made themselves odious by preaching fire, hell, and damnation in the public square. In fact, it was against the law to preach anywhere downtown. The body of Christ in Santa Fe, however, had determined that the community needed childcare. So the people of the church set up two sessions each day, when parents could bring their children to skate for $2.75 a session. The music was Christian and the workers were the church members. The USDA even donated lunches for the kids. The outcome was terrific, and every day, young people were being won to Christ in that building. The altar and pulpit were on wheels and were rolled out each Sunday morning. As a child of the seventies, I especially liked the disco ball in the church ceiling. DQ and I spent several days there being used by God and leading young people to Jesus.

While our stay at the church was wonderful, everything else seemed to fall apart. DQ's bike refused to run. The generator light stayed on until the bike lost power and died. DQ ordered a wiring harness and spent two days rewiring it. When he cranked it up, it did the exact same thing as before. My bike had to be taken to the shop, because it was blowing oil out the tailpipes – not a good sign. The shop said it needed a top end. The problem was that we had no money and no time, and the top end had just been rebuilt 300 miles earlier.

We took a day off to lighten our moods. The day was supposed to be filled with fun and adventure, but true to our calling, it became a bit of a disaster. We borrowed a pickup truck and set out to find some hot springs to soak our bones. The drive through the Jemez Mountains was incredible. It got even better as we entered the Bandelier mountain range. We even saw a bear as it sped through the birch and ponderosa pine forest.

Just when we thought things couldn't be any better, we entered the Santa Fe National Forest. We found ourselves descending 2,000 feet into Valley Grande. The size of the closed-up volcano was incredible. Soon, we arrived at the parking area. We parked, then hiked to the hot springs. DQ was quite leery about letting me hike to the springs due to my chronic pain and limitations, but I gave him no choice and assured him I could make it. I suppose it wasn't really a surprise to him when I fell down the mountain – twice. I was scraped up and sore, but became even more determined. I felt like I had earned the right to enjoy the mineral baths. DQ allowed me to continue, certain that he didn't want to deal with me in the truck if we turned back. We found a small private pool with beautiful 104-degree water. The effort was worth the outcome, and for a short time, we escaped from the troubles of the world.

The next day, we entered reality again. DQ had broken his wrist two years earlier, and had re-injured it driving the non-power-steering school bus. His wrist was all swollen, and the pain was so bad that he couldn't sleep. We went to the air force base in Albuquerque to see a doctor. I was filled with fear and apprehension. I couldn't drive the school bus and was concerned that DQ might need an operation on his wrist. The visit to the doctor yielded a wrist brace and a diagnosis of strained tendons.

The minister of the church assured us that we could stay as long as we needed, and he encouraged us to keep the ministry in focus. We deduced that we were under heavy spiritual attack and that we had to get to Sturgis. We picked up my bike, in boxes, and tied it to the trailer. We planned our departure, because we simply couldn't stay there any longer. I had been depressed since we arrived, and DQ had been a little grouchy. We felt like we would lose our sanity if we didn't get away.

As we started out of town on the interstate, the bus wouldn't go over forty miles per hour. The mountain climb out of Santa Fe was steep. If we didn't gain some speed before the climb, we knew we wouldn't make it up the mountain. We pulled to the side of the road and DQ adjusted the carburetor, but to no avail. It didn't make any sense to us, because the bus had run fine in town. Not knowing what else to do, I got on my knees and put one hand on the dash and the other on DQ's arm. I prayed out loud, and the bus picked up speed. As long as we prayed, the speedometer steadily increased. By the time we reached the top of the mountain, we were running 55 mph. That was a miracle, because the bus usually climbed hills at a steady 15 mph. At the top of the hill, it was as if we broke through a brick wall and into freedom. The evil force that had been repressing us was left behind, and we were free once again. We were free to go to Denver, where our sixth trial awaited us.

Chapter 16

Somewhere

Somewhere beyond these reasons and feelings,
Somewhere beyond the passion and fatigue,
I know You're there and that Your spirit is leading me,
Somewhere beyond all this.
— Rich Mullins, "Somewhere"

As the landscape of New Mexico faded behind us, the lush mountains of Colorado beckoned us to come. God even blessed us when we saw a herd of pronghorn. He raised our spirits with the hope of an easier, freer time. It was a nice thought, but probably highly unlikely at that point. In all fairness, some bright spots appeared at every stop. We found Christian people who looked past our rough exterior and were able to see the commonality of our mutual Savior, Jesus Christ. That fact continually gave us the courage to continue.

When we arrived at Gateway Christian Church in Aurora, Colorado, we found a large packet of mail waiting for us. As I sorted through the bills and notices, a letter from the *State of Florida, Motor Vehicle Department* caught my attention. The letter asked us to provide the reason that we had allowed our auto insurance to lapse. The letter explained that a new state law had taken effect June 1 that made it a crime punishable by a $1,000 fine, 30 days in jail, and loss of driver's license for one year. I looked at the letter again and tried to find which vehicle was being discussed, but I only found a policy number. I suspected it to be the car we sold when we left Florida, so I laid the letter aside. When I finished sorting the mail, I went inside and called the Florida motor vehicle department. When I was informed which vehicle it was, the reality of disaster number six hit me full force. The letter was regarding our bus, and DQ was wanted by the state of Florida.

I hung up and called our insurance agent. He seemed useless to us, though, which was evident by the situation in which we found ourselves. I had made a payment in January for what I thought was a full year of insurance on the bus. In reality, it had only been a six-month premium. I informed the agent, whom we had been with for years, that we needed to get the policy back in force. He refused to help us, saying that it was in the state's hands at that point. The reason was clear. They had not wanted to write the policy on the "homemade" school bus/motorhome in the first place. The only reason they had done so was because we had four other policies with them. When we sold everything we owned to go on the road, we cancelled the other policies, and only kept the bus insurance policy. The company essentially dropped us by not sending us a premium notice. DQ was once again a wanted man, and we couldn't leave Colorado knowing we were traveling illegally. It felt as if the score was Satan 1, God 0.

We felt deflated and doomed to fail. We spent the evening in prayer and in my case, in tears. During the night, though, something besides despair surfaced. We were tired of feeling whipped and sick of being defeated. We made the decision that this incident would not stop us. God had called us to Sturgis, and even if we had to walk, we would be at the Buffalo Chip Campground for the motorcycle rally the first week of August. God *had* called us, He *had* equipped us, and it would take more than the forces of hell and a spineless insurance agent to keep us from our purpose in Him.

We prayed all night and called our home church in Bayonet Point in the morning. The church secretary, Vickie, worked her way through the yellow pages, calling insurance people. Meanwhile, I called the state insurance office and filed a grievance against our agent with the state. We had received none of the three notices that were supposedly sent out, and our forwarding agents confirmed that fact. The filing of a grievance allowed us to get a binder from another company, which would keep us on the road until the matter was decided. The backlog was six months, which would allow us time to finish our tour and return home. God is good. The score was now God 1, Satan 1.

Vickie called back within the hour and had found a yes at the end of many noes. She found a company that would insure our bus. We needed a person to sign the papers, so we called our head elder and asked him to handle it for us. He was thrilled to stand in for us, and we faxed a power of attorney to him. By day's end, we were once again street legal. The final score was God 2, Satan 1. The sucker lost again!

Chapter 17

The Generator, Round Two

O Lord, who may abide in Thy tent? Who may dwell
on Thy holy hill? He who walks with integrity, and
works righteousness, and speaks truth in his heart.
(Psalm 15:1-2 NASB)

We had the refunded money from Kmart for the faulty
generator, but we still needed one to replace it. Too
many times that month, we were without power and air conditioning. We checked prices in each town, but the cost of the
generator we needed always exceeded the money we had. Now,
though, Builders Square in Denver had a wonderful, powerful
generator on sale. Their competitor had it for thirty dollars
cheaper. Builder's Square advertised that they would beat any
competitor's price by 10 percent. That would give us an additional ninety-eight-dollar discount. We decided to go for it.
Of course, going to the store, paying for the generator, loading
the new machine up, and driving away would certainly be too
much to ask for. Nothing seemed easy for DQ and Beth Roberts.

We borrowed a pickup truck, and the church secretary
agreed to go with us. We called ahead to the Edgewater store

and were told that they had what we needed. We paid for the generator at the service desk and were given the competitor's discount. I went to get the truck while DQ asked the department head to bring the generator to the front. DQ came out of the store alone and informed me that this store only had a reconditioned generator in stock. It was only forty dollars cheaper, and we didn't think that was much of a value. The manager called another store ten miles away and verified that they had a new one in stock. He told us that we could just show them the receipt and pick up the generator. So away we went with the paid-in-full receipt in hand.

When we arrived at the Southside store, we were escorted to the generator aisle. They only had one generator left, but they couldn't find the warranty paperwork. We refused that generator, because we knew it was wise to have the paperwork. The reason we had called ahead and verified the availability of the generator was to avoid any hassle. So we went to the front desk and asked for the manager, to lodge a complaint. The manager informed us that even if he had the generator, he couldn't give it to us. The other store should have refunded our money, because they couldn't swap merchandise between stores. We would have to return to the Edgewater store, get our money back, and then proceed to store number three to purchase the generator.

DQ and I looked at each other and wondered aloud why everything we did had to be this difficult. We shared our story with Scott, the service manager who was helping us. We figured that was the only possible reason God brought us to that store. We were obedient to the Holy Spirit's leading, and Scott lined everything up for us. He called the Westminster store, and they verified that a new generator, still in plastic and in the box, with paperwork, awaited us. Scott then called the Edgewater store and informed them that they blew it. He demanded that they have our money plus an additional twenty-five dollars for gas waiting for us when we arrived. We thanked Scott for his diligence and promised to pray for him.

The manager of the Edgewater store was a chicken and hid in the office. We suspected that he was afraid to deal with *the Bikers*. Scott had given us the regional manager's name, so we could file a complaint, but we figured it was all working out for God's glory. When we arrived at the Westminster store, we joked with the church secretary that we ought to visit the Fort Collins Builders Square, as it was the only one we had missed. She declined, our one-hour trip had already taken over five hours. The generator was waiting at the front of the store for us, and we were in and out of there within five minutes. We had put a total of 140 miles on two vehicles, but we were the proud parents of an awesome, power-churning machine. It would indeed serve us for years, worry free.

Chapter 18

The Long-Awaited Words

As our eleven days in Denver came to a close, we began to say goodbye to our new friends. Mark and Jean, a couple who lived near the church, had allowed us to take showers at their home whenever we needed. We also shared a few meals and desserts with them. On our last evening in Denver, Jean had my favorite dessert, peach cobbler and ice cream waiting for us. As we talked and laughed, we all wanted to avoid the inevitable. They walked outside to see us off.

It was then that Jean made the statement that we longed to hear since the conception of Christian Riders Ministry. We had dreamed of hearing it, yet the sound of the words were sweeter than we could have ever imagined. Jean said, "I want you two to know that you've changed the way we will look at bikers from now on." We praised our Lord God for allowing our lives to show that and our ears to hear that within our first year of ministry. In that moment, we truly felt that Christian Riders Ministry had been a service to our own people – our brothers and sisters of the road. Maybe some misunderstanding or prejudice had been erased, and more love could now be shown.

There are really no categories of bikers or teachers or rich or poor or blacks or whites in God's sight. We are all God's handiwork created in His image, and we should respect each other. We are all equal as human beings made in the image of a loving and righteous Father. On that day, four people stepped a little closer to the image of Christ Jesus.

Chapter 19

Disaster Number Seven

The beginning of the day gave us no indication of what the end of the day would hold, but few days do. After running a few errands in Denver, we were loaded up and pulled out into traffic by one o'clock. We left there better equipped materially for Sturgis. God had blessed us with the generator, a 10 x 20' tent, and the church had blessed us with some cash. We were stronger spiritually too. We had been tested for the six weeks prior, and passed. The encouragement we had received along the way prepared our spirits. We felt free and were bound for Sturgis. Sturgis or bust! Unfortunately, some "busting" was yet to occur.

Daylight burned quickly as the afternoon faded into evening. We pushed on east into the dimming light to a rest area just inside the Nebraska border. The prairie had stretched out for the past ninety miles with very few towns in between. The lights of the town could be seen from about ten miles out. Just as we entered town, DQ yelled, "Bikes!" Without hesitation, I leaped to my feet and fought the forward braking motion of the vehicle in order to get to the rear. When I was halfway back, I saw a shower of sparks coming from the trailer, and I quickly shouted the information back over my shoulder to DQ. He proceeded to stop the bus on a dime, and he was out the door with a fire extinguisher by the time I got back to the front. I quickly retrieved the second fire extinguisher and followed in his tracks.

The sight before us was strange and unnatural. The rear driver-side wheel of the trailer was gone. The axle, having been ground to a half-circle, sat on the pavement. By the grace of God and the hand of an angel, the bikes remained firmly attached to the trailer. They both leaned at a 45-degree angle and defied gravity. Reason quickly told us that they should have been on the pavement, scattered along the highway and ditches.

We immediately sprang into action. Time was of the utmost importance, as we were in a life or death situation. We had stopped in the slow lane of a four-lane highway, because there was no shoulder. The town speed limit sign was visible ahead, but the speed limit didn't drop until then. We had semi-trucks blowing past us at sixty-five miles per hour. And, as our luck would have it, our emergency flashers refused to blink. We didn't have any flares on board either. DQ quickly grabbed our orange construction cones and set them out near the rear of the trailer.

We worked quickly to unload both motorcycles. Whenever a truck or car approached, I quickly grabbed the flashlight and motioned the cars over into the fast lane. The first car that passed westbound turned around and brought our trailer tire back. The Good Samaritan said, "Parts are parts," and he quickly got back into his car and drove away. We laughed and commented that he could have offered to help us a little more. We managed to get the trailer unhooked from the hitch, but with the wheel missing, we couldn't get it off the road.

The next person to stop was Ronny. He tried to help us,

but the trailer wouldn't budge. He surveyed the trailer and said, "I have a motorcycle trailer that will hold two Harleys. For one hundred dollars, I'll swap you out and get you on the road tomorrow." He continued, "I'm on my way to work at the railroad, or I'd help you more now. I have to go, because the trains don't wait. There's a free campground a half mile up the road. Stay there, and I'll come by in the morning and get you fixed up." With that, Ronny was gone. It was nine o'clock, fully dark, and our junk was still scattered all over the road.

Having no choice, we continued to struggle with the trailer. We had concluded that the only possible way to get it off the road was to flip it over onto the hill that went up from the pavement. We prayed and pushed with all our might. Just then, another driver stopped to help. His extra weight and push were just what we needed to get the trailer flipped. With every inch the trailer moved, DQ and I praised God, while our anonymous helper cussed under his breath with every inch.

The next step was to get the bikes off the road and to the campground. I jumped on my Triumph, and glory to God, she cranked. The other driver followed me to the campground and then brought me back. DQ had his Shovelhead running and waiting for me to take to the campground, and he followed me in the bus.

When we got settled in, the reality hit us of what had just happened. We laughed and praised our God and Protector. Many possible scenarios played out before us as to what could have happened, but we didn't concentrate on those. Rather, our minds were set on what *did* happen. God had preserved our lives, our bikes, and our bus. He sent helpers and even provided a free campground with full hookups. The lost trailer had never really been an asset, so we didn't consider losing it to be a loss.

Another interesting thing happened that night. For the first time, we didn't allow the problem to become the main focus.

God had a plan in all of it, and tomorrow we would see exactly what that was. As for that night, sleep came quickly, and we rested in the arms of our Protector and Provider.

Chapter 20

Out of Darkness Comes Light

We awoke after a wonderful night's sleep. Perhaps it was the free campground, but it was probably the assurance of being in God's hands that allowed the renewing sleep. The events of the previous night seemed like a bad dream, but our muscles reminded us that it was not a dream. Ronny, true to his word, came and picked DQ up at nine o'clock. They spent all day together. There was a reason the wheel came off where it did. It turned out that God had gone to a lot of trouble to line the events up.

That night, Ronny pulled out of his driveway later than usual, on his way to work the midnight shift on the railroad. He was late, because he had just had a fight with Kim, his wife. According to Ronny, their fighting had become commonplace lately – at least since his wife discovered Ronny's unfaithfulness when she was diagnosed with a venereal disease. The couple had even discussed divorce, but little Ronny, age six, and Tina, age three, seemed to delay the issue. If Ronny would have left for work on time, our paths would have never crossed. That would have been a great tragedy, because Ronny and Kim had no one in their lives to help them through their pain, and their children's futures hung in the balance.

While DQ was at Ronny's house, I received a visit from a local police officer. The knock on the bus door alarmed me, but the sight of the man in the blue uniform really shook me up. My greatest fear was that something had happened to my beloved DQ. The officer quickly informed me that he knew nothing about DQ, but was in fact looking for me. He questioned me about the trailer and informed me that it was illegal in their state not to report a wreck. The police officer also told me that the trailer had been illegally left on the right of way.

I explained the accident and the frantic details of the prior evening. The police officer informed me that the accident report had been filed, and we had twenty-four hours to remove the trailer. Perhaps it was the rattletrap, old school bus, or perhaps it was my weariness, but whatever the reason, the officer gave me two warning tickets and didn't take me to the jailhouse. He was more than pleased to let me know how kind he was being to me. I was just glad to play the humble servant part and get rid of the man in blue. Relief washed over me as his car pull out. Gone were the days when a blue light brought paranoia, but I still didn't feel at ease with the police.

Ronny dropped DQ off that evening on his way to the railroad. He had a better motorcycle trailer at his house that he was willing to sell us for fifty dollars. It needed tires, but those could be obtained for forty dollars. He agreed to let us keep the new taillights, spare tire, and toolbox from our old trailer. We prayed about the deal all night and had peace about it. It would have cost us around one hundred dollars to fix our old broken trailer, and even then, it wouldn't have been much of a trailer. It was settled, then. DQ would finish up the trailer deal the next day. We also prayed all night that Kim would make herself available to us, so the real reason we were detained here could be dealt with.

The second day, the floodgates opened up and true ministry took place. DQ shared with Ronny and Kim all day. He shared about our life B.C. (before Christ) and about the pain and agony we had put each other through. DQ shared how Jesus had not only saved our souls, but how He also saved our lives and marriage. Many people had endured less than we had and lost it all. The reason we hadn't been divorced was only because of God's great love and mercy.

Ronny said that he couldn't believe how well we had handled the accident. We never got upset, never swore, and never questioned. We knew without a doubt that God had His hand in all of it, and we would come out the victors. Kim told us how she saw Jesus Christ in our actions. It was enough for them, and they recommitted themselves and their children to Jesus. As we pulled away, Ronny and Kim stood with their arms around each other, waving goodbye. Truly, those events were God's handiwork, His great healing on a major hurt. Our Father God restored all things.

Chapter 21

South Dakota at Last

Stop being deceived; God is not to be ridiculed. A person harvests whatever he plants. (Galatians 6:7 ISV)

On July 24, 1992, we pulled into the town of Sturgis, South Dakota, for the first time. That day was significant to us, because all we had done since our ordination built up to that point. The hounds of hell had sought to discourage us on many occasions, so we wouldn't arrive there. They failed to accomplish their objective, and they would stand before their master to await punishment. For our part, we remained focused on the task at hand, and God hadn't failed to deliver us to the promised destination. We had no idea what the next few weeks would hold, but we knew without a shadow of a doubt that we had been raised up for such a time as this. While we knew that we had succeeded, we also knew instinctively that the war had only just begun. We had won the first of many battles, but many upcoming battles would leave us holding on for dear life, with only our faith intact. God had brought us to that point, and He would carry us forward. We had renewed courage and power resulting from our ever-growing faith in Christ and the knowledge that He who began a good work in us would carry it on to completion (Philippians 1:6).

We were elated as we pulled the school bus and open trailer into the parking lot of Sturgis Christian Church. We sat in the yard with the pastor and his wife and listened as Pastor John talked for an hour and a half. He told us in no uncertain terms that he disliked the motorcycle rally, the vendors, the bikers, and the way the town prostituted itself to the multi-million-dollar event. We let him talk until he was finished. Then it was DQ's turn. He calmly objected to what the pastor had said. DQ countered that every August, God brought a mission field to the Christians of Sturgis. Instead of retreating, because they found the bikers revolting, the Christian response should be to pray, love, and seek to make a difference at every level of the rally. At the close of the evening, we all knew that a friendship had begun, and that in one short week, ministry opportunities would abound.

The pastor offered to allow us to set up our 10 x 20' tent in the churchyard. The lot was located just a few blocks off Main Street, but since we had never attended the rally before, we weren't sure if we could attract folks that far. After prayer, we knew that God hadn't changed His mind. Since Daytona, when a fellow vender had mentioned the campground, we knew where we were supposed to be. While we prayed, God also made it clear to us that we were supposed to end the jewelry trade as a cover for ministry. We were to tell the campground owner that we were Christians who had come to minister, and we sold jewelry on the side.

DQ and I prayed all evening. The next day, we went east of town to locate "the Chip" – the notorious Buffalo Chip Campground. We were told that the owner wasn't in, and we should come back the next day. After four days of being told the same thing, we waited for the man. It didn't surprise us when

Woody showed up twenty minutes later. He said, "Come back and see me tomorrow, so I can think about it." After six more days of seeing the man every day, he finally agreed to allow us to set up the ministry tent for $145, instead of the regular vending fee of $450. We were also told that in the Chip's eleven-year history, they had never had a Christian tent there. We were grateful, and believed that God had touched the owner's heart. That was the ministry we had come from Florida to do. We would realize in later years, it was what God had in mind as one of the high points of Christian Riders Ministry. Yet, it's where we would face our heaviest persecutions and trials. That's where we would shine like diamonds for Jesus Christ, our Lord and Savior. However, a lot of compression must happen to coal before the diamond shines.

When God's people have victory, the demons aren't far behind. As we pulled out of the Chip after securing our spot, I heard a weird noise from DQ's bike, like it was running underwater. I looked back, saw the problem, shook my head, and gave him the sign to kill the engine. When DQ asked me why I had him kill his engine, I said, "You'll have to see this one." His tailpipe hadn't just fallen off. That would have meant a new five-dollar clamp and a few minutes of repair work. No, nothing was that easy for us. The flange on the cylinder head that held the clamp and pipe to the engine had broken. It meant we either needed a new cylinder head or a really good welder. We located a new cylinder head that cost $250. We certainly didn't have that much money, so we found a great welder who fixed it for forty-one dollars. This meant DQ had to rebuild the top of the engine in the tent. The dust was fierce at the Chip so everything had to stay wrapped in plastic wrap until it was assembled. He did this in one afternoon and it was a witness to many of the bikers. We were soon riding again. Thank you, Jesus!

Chapter 22

A New Breed of Bikers: Christians

Look how good and how pleasant it is when brothers live together in unity! (Psalm 133:1 ISV)

The campgrounds at Sturgis were known for free-flowing alcohol and nudity. In short, they were known for sex, drugs, and rock and roll. The Buffalo Chip Campground was no different than many of the competing campgrounds. The Chip did something different in 1992, though. They were the first to have a Christian ministry within the camp. We set the CRM tent up just inside the amphitheater. It was the first thing people drove by upon entering. The location was great for us, but brought mixed emotions from the campers. Some loudly questioned why we were let in, because we spoiled their fun or made them feel guilty. With our presence, conviction from God fell on the campground. There was no surprise in that. We used to be just like many of those people. A few years earlier, we would have taken part in the debauchery. Yet, on Saturday, August 8, 1992, we set up the 10 x 20' tent for Jesus Christ for the first time. The tent officially opened at 9:00 a.m. on Sunday morning for worship and communion. It would be open every day until August 16 for daily morning worship.

The eight-day event was filled with twenty-hour days, little sleep, and included many trials, temptations, and hard-learned lessons. Some people came in to heckle, some to talk, some to scoff, and some to persecute. We attempted to pour out love to each one. God sent friends to encourage us, and Satan sent others to make us fall. However, people were touched, led to the Lord, and baptized into Christ.

The night before the tent opened, we went into town to attend a tent revival meeting held by the Christian Crusaders Motorcycle Club, a group from Washington state. We needed to get fired up at the revival, so we could give back spiritually to folks at the Chip. Words could never describe the encouragement that meeting was to us. We found out that we weren't the only sold-out, hardcore bikers attempting to make an impact in the scooter world. We were energized for ministry. The leader of Christian Crusaders, Preacher Mike, had ministry leaders from each group stand up and tell who they were and where they were set up to do ministry. Since DQ was vertically challenged, he stood on a chair in order to be seen. Preacher Mike said, "Little Buddy, who are you and where are you serving?"

DQ answered, "DQ Roberts and my bride, Beth, and we have a tent ministry at the Buffalo Chip Campground."

You could have heard a pin drop. Preacher Mike just stared at DQ before getting a huge grin on his face and a twinkle in his eyes. "I want to talk to you after service," Mike proclaimed. The leaders of the other groups announced where they were from and where they were ministering. Of the eight groups, only two of us were set up in a location to minister.

The events of the night kept us from talking to Preacher Mike afterwards. During the altar call, he had the leaders come forward to pray with folks who needed it. I stayed in my seat and begged God to allow DQ to minister to someone. I wanted a blessing for him so badly. When I looked up, the men on both sides of DQ were praying with someone, but DQ just stood there. My heart ached. Preacher Mike brought three people forward and had them repeat their confession of Jesus Christ as their Lord and Savior. Then he went on to urge the three of them to get baptized as soon as they could. DQ reached up and touched Preacher Mike on the elbow. He whispered in Mike's ear, "I have the keys to a church three blocks away. Let's get it done now."

Mike's eyes lit up. He could hardly believe a tramp like DQ had the keys to a church in Sturgis. After the closing prayer, he announced that we would all walk across Main Street to the baptisms. What an incredible sight. Fifty fuzzy bikers walked down the overflowing streets of Sturgis singing, "This Little Light of Mine."

The crowds stopped and parted, mouths agape with disbelief. Preacher Mike and DQ led the procession. My prayer had been answered far beyond my wildest dreams; DQ got to minister. The band of singing bikers quickly filled the small church. A brother helped himself to the piano and beat out a tune. The church rocked like it hadn't rocked in years, and the Holy Spirit filled the small building. We threw the windows open, and the music filled the night. The three baptisms were incredible. Preacher Mike closed in prayer, thanking God for the night, the souls saved, and for a church in that town open to bikers.

When I looked up after the prayer, I saw Pastor John, the pastor of the church, standing in the rear of his church with tears streaming down his face. The little adobe church had not been overflowing for many years. John told us that he had heard the music many blocks away. He told us later that he had been incredibly blessed by our arrival. He admitted that, because of us, he had been able to tear down some self-imposed walls and prejudices. He once again realized that his ministry was supposed to be to all people. That night, Satan lost a foothold, and the religious walls around the town of Sturgis began to crumble.

It would be six years before we would find out why Mike reacted as he did when he found out where we set up our tent. The story began at Sturgis in August of 1989. Preacher Mike had the Buffalo Chip on his heart as a place to do ministry, but none of his team wanted anything to do with the campground. So he took his team out to the Chip to walk the perimeter, and he prayed that God would raise up someone to minister there, because the need was so great. DQ and I gave our lives to the Lord nine months later, in May 1990. During the next two Augusts, in 1990 and 1991, the Crusaders walked the boundaries. They prayed for the lost there and asked God to raise up a warrior to come minister. In 1990, while the Crusaders walked and prayed, God was discipling us. One month after the Crusaders' 1991 walk, on September 29, we were ordained into full-time ministry. Before Preacher Mike and his group could go out to the Chip in 1992, God sent two warriors – a little biker and his bride – to be an answer to their prayers. We would spend eleven years at the Chip and touch tens of thousands of lives, all because of one man's vision, the prayers of his group, and the faithfulness of the Lord Jesus Christ.

Chapter 23

His Great Faithfulness

Come, you who are blessed of My Father, inherit the kingdom prepared for you from the foundation of the world. For I was hungry, and you gave Me something to eat; I was thirsty, and you gave Me something to drink; I was a stranger, and you invited Me in. (Matthew 25:34-35 NASB)

W e awoke the next morning with the amazement of the previous night still lifting our spirits. Based upon what had happened so far, we knew the rest of the week would be dramatic. We held a worship service at the Chip for the first time in history on Sunday, August 4, 1992. People passed by and stared in wonder, or heckled us. That was difficult for us. But when five people showed up for the service, we poured ourselves out in song and word, DQ playing the guitar, for them. Just one person would have been a blessing to us, but God blessed us with five. We knew that each person was lavishly loved by God. Before the week was over, three of those five would leave as new persons in Christ. The other two were already believers.

Monday was slow, except for the visit from our new friends.

We held worship every morning at 9:00 a.m. A few people came by to talk, but mostly we felt like circus freaks at a sideshow. Most people walked by and laughed at us, called us names, or heckled us. At the previous night's service, we met Steve and Carolyn Ervin, a couple from North Carolina who were the founders of His Laboring Few Motorcycle Ministry. As soon as Carolyn heard DQ speak, she said, "That boy's from North Carolina, like us." They found us in the crowd, and we became fast friends. We were overjoyed when they pulled up late in the afternoon at the Chip. Just being around them lifted our spirits. They had a testimony close to ours in many ways. A bond was formed that would last a lifetime.

We made a mistake that evening, and God was quick to reveal it to us. We left the Chip and went into town for the Crusaders' revival meeting. We enjoyed it, but it lacked the blessing of the previous night. We both knew that we weren't where we belonged. God had given us a field to work at the Chip, and we were feeding ourselves instead of ministering to others. We couldn't get away fast enough, determined that the rest of the days and nights would be different. We would work our field and wouldn't leave unless God specifically told us to do so.

God began to reveal something else to me that night. It was something that then, in my spiritual infancy, I thought God and I would easily overcome. How wrong I was. It would take many years for God to break my independent spirit and teach me biblical submission to my husband. One of my greatest blessings was that DQ would never demand it of me, but he would always encourage me to be the best in God that I could be. He explained to me that biblical submission had to be freely given or it was worth little to the receiver. The biker world is a very male-dominated society. My parents had raised me to be independent and to not need anyone. Since DQ was fourteen years my senior, I respected him and mostly heeded his advice. But

I was still very much my own woman and took care of myself. That presented a problem. There were several times that week when I refused DQ's direction for me. It caused disunity in our marriage and in the ministry. It was very difficult for me, because I had never seen biblical submission modeled.

As strong as our conviction had been at the Crusaders' tent on Sunday night to stay at the Chip from then on, two full days and nights of ridicule and ostracism took its toll on our resolve. By Wednesday, we were sure that if we didn't get away for a while, we wouldn't survive the week. Every morning we served coffee and held a worship time; every morning DQ preached his sermon to me alone. Even though I listened with all my soul, the days tore at our hearts. Steve and Carolyn came several times to encourage us, as they hadn't set up a ministry tent. Instead, they went wherever God led them to help. We asked them if we could tag along with them on Wednesday and help minister. We thought that together we could talk to folks and share some tips, making us all stronger. We planned to be back at our tent in the evening, so we could minister during the later, busier hours.

The couple informed us that they felt led by God to go and witness at the Waylon Jennings/Willie Nelson concert. The tickets were twenty dollars per person. DQ let them know that we couldn't afford to go, so maybe another day would work better. Steve insisted on giving us the forty dollars. So DQ quickly adjusted his motorcycle and off we roared, without prayer. We got about a mile down the road when DQ's Shovelhead died. We all stopped, and DQ handed the money back. Steve and Carolyn refused the money. They told us to go get the church van (which had been left at the Chip for our use) and meet them at the concert. We went back for the van and trailer, so we could get DQ's bike off the road. When we finally got the bike back to the campground, DQ said that he didn't think we should go to the concert, and I agreed. God had put us in the campground, and we continued to fight against His will. DQ admitted that he had really wanted to see the concert, so it became his desire against God's will. Once again, we had refused to be still and listen to God. We humbled ourselves in the tent and begged God to break our hearts for the people, just as His heart was broken for us. Then we opened the tent for ministry, and God gave us many great witnessing opportunities. Lives were changed that night, as God intended.

We decided we needed to be available in the evenings and nights, as well as in the mornings. We set up a fresh pot of coffee. That alone brought over about two dozen people. We attempted to make every word count for Christ. Around ten in the evening, a couple pulled up in front of the tent and turned off their bike. They came inside and explained to us that they wanted to renew their wedding vows. We gave them some brief biblical marriage counseling, which they appreciated. Then DQ went and cleared it with Woody, the owner. He said we could use the stage at 12:10 a.m., after the band was done. At 12:10, DQ and I walked onto the stage with the couple and read Scripture in front of about 8,500 highly-intoxicated bikers. To our absolute amazement, the crowd stood respectfully and watched, as we renewed the couple's commitment. I wished I could have glimpsed into the spiritual realm right then. I believe I would've seen about 8,500 angels holding their hands over the biker's mouths. We ended with prayer before walking off the stage to the biker applause of revving engines. All doubts were gone. We could hide no more. The Christian Riders were now at the Chip and being used by God. Thank you, Jesus.

That night, we did real ministry. I took a homeless couple into the bus and fed them dinner, because they were out of food and money. Another very young couple came into the tent. They were both Christians who loved Jesus, but they hadn't kept themselves pure, and the girl was pregnant. DQ talked to Bob while I spoke to Daphne. They were rightly worried about their witness. Bob was consumed with guilt, and Daphne was ashamed.

I counseled Daphne in the bus while DQ ministered to Bob in the tent. DQ encouraged Bob to repent and then let his parents, pastor, and God help them with their future. I reminded Daphne that life was sacred, and she quickly told me she wouldn't abort the child. We talked about her options, and I gave her the same advice DQ had given Bob. I told her that repentance was in order and that they needed to stand on God's Word, because the Lord is faithful to forgive.

They left encouraged and planned to meet with their parents and youth pastor, hoping to receive the blessing of their parents and pastor before they got married. We were blessed to be used by God to offer hope to Bob and Daphne. We still felt unworthy to minister to others, for who were we that God would heed our call? We were His servants – nothing more, nothing less.

Chapter 24

Unequally Yoked

*My brethren, if any among you strays from the truth
and one turns him back, let him know that he who
turns a sinner from the error of his way will save his
soul from death and will cover a multitude of sins.*
(James 5:19-20 NASB)

Everyone has needs. Some people are just more honest about their needs than others.

We were up at seven, after just six hours of sleep. At morning worship, it was again just DQ and me. It was hard to stand up and lead worship with just the two of us there. We both sang harmony as DQ played his Gibson guitar. Then DQ preached, and we served each other communion. It was all done with the world, or at least *our* world, watching and ridiculing. Although we felt out of place when it was just the two of us, we had announced over the campground PA system that we would have a church service at 9:00 a.m., so we made the decision to be faithful to God and our peers.

After the service, we took the Sturgis Christian Church van into town, so we could take showers and do laundry at Pastor

John's house. When we got back, we opened up the tent. A couple came in who wanted us to marry them. We sensed that there was more to the story. It didn't take long for us to find out that Erik was a Baptist pastor's son and Pam was a Mormon. The more we talked to them, the louder God shouted "No!" in our ears. Erik was full of guilt and Pam was very controlling. She refused to be married by Erik's father or any other Baptist pastor, but said that she would allow us to perform the wedding ceremony. Pam said that she had been baptized as a Mormon against her will. As we talked, however, she admitted that she believed the *Book of Mormon*. Then, she admitted to being a fourth-generation Mormon. When she stated that they wanted to have kids immediately, Erik's eyes got big and he said, "Well, maybe not immediately." That caused us more concern.

I got Pam away from Erik, so DQ could talk to him. DQ told him how the Mormon church sometimes seemed to use women and children against men to trap them in church-controlled marriages. He emphasized to Erik that his relationship with Pam was not one of being equally yoked. They talked about Erik's faith for about twenty minutes, while I shared Jesus Christ with Pam. Erik said he didn't want to give up his relationship with Jesus, but instead wanted to rededicate his life to Jesus right then, which he did. Erik thanked DQ and said he was going home to his family. My attempt to share Jesus with Pam proved unsuccessful, but at least she heard the Word of God. Pam stormed out and demanded that Erik leave with her. He refused and sat there into the evening talking with DQ. When Erik left, he left alone, heading home to his family.

Chapter 25

Creatures of the Night

We saw him as he made a beeline for the tent, stumbling, yet coming in at a fast pace. DQ and I looked at each other in apprehension and gave our usual warning in unison, "Incoming." The man's entire demeanor warned of trouble. His hair was wild, greasy, and matted. He wore tattered, stained jeans and a ripped t-shirt. His smell preceded him by five feet. His arms were cut, and he had bloodstains on his clothes. What really gave his problem away, though, were his eyes. They were glassed over and darted back and forth like he was in danger from every angle, as if he was a caged animal ready to lash out.

We were totally exhausted by that point in the week. Seven days of ministering while sleeping only four to six hours a night had taken its toll on us. While our bodies were physically exhausted, we were prayed up and spiritually alert. The power of the Holy Spirit was strong in us and in the tent. DQ stood at the front of tent, yet the man rushed past him and sat down next to me in the horseshoe of chairs. It was a position neither DQ nor I wanted to be in, but propriety kept me seated. The man opened his mouth, and the vileness of hell poured forth. His gravel-like, deep, dark, rumbling voice reverberated throughout the tent as he spewed his first round of curses. First, he cursed God, then he cursed DQ, and finally he cursed me. DQ would break in and say, "God loves you, and I love you, and we can tell you how your suffering can end." Then the circle would begin again.

Every once in a while, the man's eyes cleared up and he would say in a pleasant, calm voice, "You know, you two are doing a great thing here." Then he would violently shake his head and begin cursing again.

Finally, DQ firmly said, "Listen, you can curse me all you want, and my Jesus can take care of Himself. But I'm not putting up with you cursing my sweet wife any longer!" The man's eyes cleared again and he seemed to understand, but then the demons began their viciousness again. Each time he paused, DQ told him of the Savior and Lord Jesus Christ and how He could bring him peace and healing and comfort. DQ told him the story about the demon-possessed man and the freedom Jesus had given to him. The man listened with a faraway look in his eyes, and then became even more agitated and began the blasphemy again. Meanwhile, I asked Jesus to bind the demon in our midst and give deliverance to this poor man.

At that point, another man came over to the Bible table. So I was able to gently get up and move away, thanking God for the opportunity. The man at the table introduced himself as Russ. He was dressed in brown leather and looked like he didn't belong there at all. I served him a cup of coffee as he told me that he felt sorry for the man in the tent. We heard the obscenities behind us as DQ kept saying, "Let me just pray for you, and it will be better." The man screeched, "No!" and spewed more profanities.

Russ and I talked about Jesus and the Scriptures. I asked him if he knew Jesus, but he dodged the question. Russ knew both the Old and New Testaments well. We shared back and forth, greatly encouraging one another. We talked for about twenty minutes until I heard the man in the tent scream, "DON'T DO THAT! DON'T PRAY!" The man rushed out with his arms flailing as he went. When I turned around, Russ had disappeared. I looked out into the night, but couldn't see him.

I straightened the Bibles and pondered what had just happened. I heard DQ's voicing saying, "Meet my wife," so I turned and looked at him as he looked at me.

I asked, "Meet who?"

DQ responded, "Did you not just see those two women in white?" I shook my head no and DQ said, "They were here when I turned to you. You had to see them." We both looked around our unobstructed view of the amphitheater that surrounded us. All we saw was black leather. He said, "They were just here. The ladies told me we were doing exactly what we were called to do, and they smiled as I turned to you. How could they just disappear when wearing all white is so obvious in this crowd? You could tell they didn't belong here and could be in danger. Now they're gone. I still can't believe you didn't see them."

I told DQ, "Surely, we've been visited by angels just now, and they fear nothing here."

We both knew that after we weren't able to help the demon-possessed man, the angels had come to encourage us. We hugged, got down on our knees in the middle of the tent, and prayed for the man. We did in prayer what we couldn't do in person – bind the demons inside him and ask God for his deliverance.

As we got up, David, a man who worked security, stepped out of the darkness and into the tent. We had tried all week to witness to David, but with no success. As he stepped into the light, David said, "Hi, Preacher. I know you wouldn't defend yourself if he attacked you, but I want you to know that I have your back. You two are doing a good thing, and I will protect you, because I know you won't protect yourselves."

DQ said, "I can't love them and beat on them. I choose to love them and leave the outcome to God."

David said, "Well, your God may use me, then, to deliver you."

David had heard and seen everything that happened the past thirty minutes. He walked over to the Bible table and asked which Bible was best for him and where he should begin reading. He took the Bible and came back to talk with us on Saturday.

DQ shared the gospel with him. He told him about the Savior and Lord who was born fully God and fully man. DQ told David how Jesus had lived a perfect life, something we were totally unable to do. God, as a righteous judge, demanded perfection. Without that perfection, we would be found guilty and consigned to an eternity of torture without Him. The good news was that Jesus paid the price on the cross that we were unable to pay. His sacrifice meant that we could live forever with God in paradise. To receive the precious free gift of salvation by grace, we just had to believe in Jesus and what He did for us on the cross. Then, we needed to turn from our sin and look at sin like God does, as rebellion. Next, we had to confess out loud that Jesus is the Christ, the Son of the living God. Once we turned from our sin and turned to Jesus, baptism would be an expression of our death to the old life and the joy of the new life. God would then give us the gift of the Holy Spirit to lead and guide us. That's the gospel message.

Then DQ asked David where he stood and if he was ready to trust in Jesus as his Lord and Savior. David told DQ he knew that was the most important decision of his life, and he wanted to think about it. DQ shook his hand and promised to be there for him. He also cautioned David not to wait too long. We saw David reading His Bible several times that weekend, and he often came to talk with us in the tent when he was off duty. He was also part of our Sunday worship congregation. "I'm going to make it," he said.

We saw David in St. Louis a while later, and he was still reading his Bible and attempting to live it. He had given his life to Jesus Christ. He was attending a local church and planning his baptism. I guess our witnessing that night in the tent could be called "ricochet" witnessing, because it seemed to bounce off the demon-possessed man and ended up reaching David. We thought we were trying to reach the demon-possessed man and Russ, and indeed we were. But David heard and responded. *Let the person who has ears to hear, listen!* (Mark 4:9 ISV).

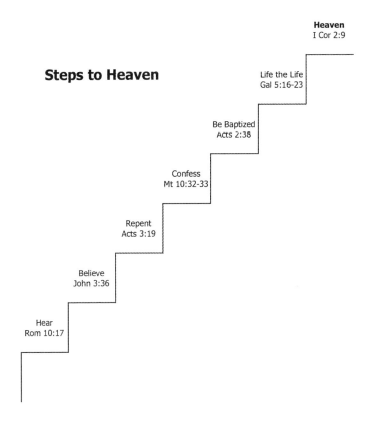

Steps to Heaven

Hear
Rom 10:17

Believe
John 3:36

Repent
Acts 3:19

Confess
Mt 10:32-33

Be Baptized
Acts 2:38

Life the Life
Gal 5:16-23

Heaven
I Cor 2:9

Chapter 26

Peace Be with You

And whatever house you enter, first say, "Peace be to this house." And if a man of peace is there, your peace will rest upon him; but if not, it will return to you. (Luke 10:5-6 NASB)

The alarm rang at 7:00 a.m., and we both groaned. I tried to open my eyes, but couldn't. I reached up and found that my eyelids really were stuck closed. DQ told me to relax while he got a wet washcloth to clean the goop from my eyelashes. I was finally able to open my eyes, but had difficulty seeing through the film over both eyes. I dressed and headed to the medic tent. The medic washed both eyes out and informed me that my eyes were infected due to the high alkaline ground here at the Chip. Lovely. It seemed to be a common problem, though. The medic graciously sent me back to the bus with supplies to wash my eyes out three times a day.

The day went by slowly for us in the tent. We were the only ones at our church service again, but we knew record crowds would be there that evening, because the band Stray Cats was scheduled to perform. We shut down the tent between two and four in the afternoon, so we could take a nap and be our best that night. We had reached the point where we could sleep through the bands, motorcycles, and anything else. I think it's called exhaustion.

The night cranked into high gear as approximately 22,000 people poured into the outdoor amphitheater. We talked to at least three dozen people between eight in the evening and one in the morning. At about ten-thirty that night, a lady entered the tent. She asked, "Is there not something you can do? Those girls on stage are underage! The scum gets them drunk, strips them down, and parades them onstage." I told her we had the power of prayer. She stormed away, mumbling. That was the horrible part of being there. The minors snuck in or showed fake IDs at the gate. Because of that, the bikers got blamed. Ultimately, it was the parents' responsibility to stop such action, but we hoped our presence would turn some of the youth back.

Our last guest of the night was Tony. He came in for coffee and was pleased to see a Christian tent there. Tony said he was Catholic, and though he and his family attended mass every Sunday, he considered his belief to be private. He said he was a good father to his four children, a good husband, and a good man in general. We asked him whom he trusted for his salvation, and he answered, "Jesus."

DQ said, "Even Jesus said, 'Why do you call me good? No one is good except God alone.'"

Tony thought about that and replied, "But I am good in doing what the Bible says."

I then mentioned to Tony, "But if God is the only one good and He is perfect, then we have to be perfect to measure up to Him."

Tony replied, "Well, I am not perfect. What should I do?"

DQ answered, "We acknowledge that Jesus took all our shortcomings and sins on the cross so we could be forgiven, and when we belong to Him, we are under His covering. Through Jesus' blood, we are forgiven for everything, and God sees us as perfect."

Tony said, "I believe that." We asked Tony if he believed that Jesus was the Christ, the Son of the living God, and his Lord and Savior. He confirmed he did, and then got up to leave.

"God bless you," we said to him.

Tony responded, "That means a lot, because I know you mean it. I don't say it much, because most say it and don't mean it."

DQ said, "Say it anyways. Jesus said, 'If you say "Peace be with you," and it is not accepted, then the peace will return to you.'"

Tony's eyes lit up, and he added, "I'll remember that. Peace be with you, brother DQ, and with you also, my friend."

Chapter 27

Jesus Is the Answer

Every man did that which was right in his own eyes.
(Judges 17:6 KJV)

Satan's obvious presence with the possessed man hadn't worked, so he sent a more subtle form of rejection. We had just set foot in the tent when Keith came in to talk. He unloaded his story without much prompting. He grew up in a Christian home but had "grown above it." His higher belief was a mixture of Christianity, reincarnation, and New Age teaching – a mixture he had created on his own. The problem compounded itself as he changed his belief to fit the questions we asked him. First, he denied the existence of hell. Then that changed when we asked why everything had an opposite in the created world, yet heaven had none. Then he said there was a hell, but since we didn't have a body, there could be no eternal torment. We explained that we will have resurrected bodies as we all live eternally; the question is *where* we will live. "That's just your doctrine!" Keith proclaimed.

I've noticed that people only use that argument when they have no other answers. Keith kept saying, "I have an open mind, and I learn by talking," but he wouldn't admit he was inconsistent.

We were still talking with Keith when Steve and Carolyn pulled up. *Yeah! Reinforcements!* I thought. We motioned for them to come over. Steve and DQ talked with Keith for another hour and a half, but it seemed as if they weren't getting through to him, and he was becoming more frustrating than the demon-possessed man from the night before. Finally, DQ and Steve called the wives over and we ended it by praying. Keith held hands with us and prayed, as well. When he left, all we could do was pray that we had planted some seeds and had thrown a monkey wrench into some of his mental gears.

The Lord often sent us someone to encourage us after particularly difficult tasks or opportunities. After Steve and Carolyn left, Chip came to the tent. He told us he was a recovering alcoholic and had been through Alcoholics Anonymous, but he found little comfort in their higher power. Chip explained that he had been praying and seeking the God of the Bible and felt led to come to the Chip to seek two people out. What a responsibility we had. We told him that the only higher power was Jesus Christ, and power was in His name alone. We explained that the God of the Bible was true, and that His Son had come to live a perfect life, die for sinners like us, and be raised from the dead. We continued to talk, realizing Chip was familiar with the Bible. Chip accepted Jesus and was baptized that night, as was another man. Chip left us with a blessing. He said, "I will see you again next year, and you will have a success story."

It's God's success story. All glory is His.

Chapter 28

What an Ending

Behold how good and pleasant it is for brothers to dwell together in unity! (Psalm 133:1 NASB)

At last, Sunday – the final day. It had been one o'clock in the morning when we closed the tent and went to sleep. Then about two hours later came a knock on the door. A hurting, hardcore biker wanted to talk to DQ about Jesus. DQ loved on him and shared Christ for about an hour. All that time, I was on my knees in prayer for them. After only a couple hours of sleep, 7:00 a.m. came. DQ and I awoke sore, groggy, and felt like we had just gone to sleep. It had been a long eight days, but God was glorified, and that made all the difference.

We prepped the tent for worship. We always got the coffee ready first, as people were eager for it. No one else had coffee for the poor masses. We planned to have communion that morning. With no fancy communion servers, we put the bread on blue, tin, cowboy plates and poured the juice into Styrofoam cups. I brought DQ's guitar from the bus, and he tuned it as I chose the music. Finally, it was time to begin. Steve and Carolyn came to worship with us, as did David. We sang songs we thought everyone would know: "Jesus Loves Me" and "This Little Light of Mine."

The Holy Spirit was present in our praises. DQ preached an encouraging and challenging sermon. We thanked God for each person we talked with during the week. I recorded some of their stories in my journal, but many more weren't written down. I was too busy most days to write, but each story was important and part of the reason we had been sent by God to Sturgis.

Our greatest joy is that our names are written in heaven (Luke 10:20).

The campground was clearing out quickly, so we began packing up. Steve and Carolyn had an engagement, so it was just me and DQ. We moved slowly, but we were moving. It took us about three hours to get everything packed. It took so long because there were still people who needed to be loved on and encouraged in Jesus' name. We said goodbye to everyone and drove the three miles to the Christian church in Sturgis. The first thing we did was take showers to get the dirt and grime off us. My eyes were better, but still infected; we figured they would heal faster now that the air was clearer. After our showers, we slept for a few hours.

The Christian Crusaders were holding a communion service at 7:00 p.m., and we wanted to attend. We grabbed a burger at the Road Kill Cafe, then headed to the Crusaders' tent. Only about two dozen people were there, and we were all tired. It was an emotional service as the men, including DQ and Steve, passed out the bread and juice. Most of us ended up on our face before God. We thanked Him for using us and begged Him to forgive us for our many shortcomings and sins. We let go of the week and our failures and came clean before God. Then we partook of the bread and juice as one body.

Mike took the pulpit but looked troubled. He shut his eyes and stood quiet before God for a couple of minutes. His silence created much energy and expectation in the tent. Mike called "Tarheel" (Steve) up to tell about a conversion they had both been involved with. Mike called Crusader Kevin up next and whispered something in his ear, and Kevin said, "I'll be right back."

Mike made small talk about the week while we waited. When Kevin returned, he handed Mike something, but no one could see what it was. Before Kevin made it to his chair, Mike replied, "I said three."

Kevin said, "But…"

Mike cut him off with a curt, "I know what I'm doing!"

Kevin left again and returned, pressing something into Mike's hand. Finally, Mike looked satisfied. He began, "We don't give out patches for nothing. You cannot buy them. We have never made a habit of giving people badges to wear. The few who do wear them have them for good reasons. Come up here, you two," Mike said, motioning to DQ and me.

We were both shocked. We did not expect that. Mike was a hardcore biker, and most of the hardcore bikers we knew seemed to think women were a little less important than men. All week long, Mike preached about how men were the priests of the ministry and of their families, while women were to be submissive to their husbands. Knowing this, I stepped slightly behind DQ's shoulder. I wanted to be the supportive wife and bring honor to DQ by being submissive in spirit.

Mike said to us, "This means a lot to us. How about wearing this over your heart? This shows unity from the west coast of the United States to the east coast." Then Mike pressed a Crusader Support Patch into DQ's palm. I was proud of DQ, but my surprise was yet to come. After DQ nodded his head and accepted his patch, Mike turned to me and said, "I got one for you, too, sister." The sparkle in his eye told me that I was the first women to ever receive that patch. Mike knew how much it meant to me by the tears in my eyes (I refused to cry!). Then Mike called Steve and Carolyn up. Steve had been given a patch earlier in the week. Mike smiled at them, looked at Carolyn, and again said, "I got one for you, too, little sister."

Mike then had all the Crusaders come up and lay hands on us. Mike anointed us with oil, and the Crusaders prayed for all aspects of our lives, from our marriages to the ministry. Steve closed by summing it up. "When I accepted this patch," he said, "it meant that I was committed to pray for Christian Crusaders, but it means more than that. If they call and need anything, whether physically, spiritually, financially, or emotionally, I will meet that need if at all possible. I will be there for them." We all hugged and gave each other a holy kiss.

God worked in many hearts that week. When we first met Preacher Mike of the Christian Crusaders, we realized that he loved bikers but didn't seem too accepting of the church crowd. For seven straight days, I prayed that God would soften Mike's heart toward churches and church people. I fervently prayed that he would understand that a church had sent us and was in full support of Christian Riders Ministry. I prayed he would recognize that Sturgis Christian Church had opened its doors to us and to all the bikers. God answered my prayers. In Mike's closing prayer, he asked the Lord to help him love religious people more freely. What a way to end a week of ministry. Thank you, Jesus.

Chapter 29

The Clean Up

Much to my dismay, I awoke Monday at 9:00 a.m. I really wanted to sleep until noon, but I couldn't seem to fall back asleep. Instead, I grabbed my Bible and studied in bed until noon. DQ had gotten up and read his Bible early, as usual, and was busy sewing the Crusader Support patches onto our vests. Steve and Carolyn had visited us all week at the campground, so we went to find *them*, since they were heading back to North Carolina in the morning. We found them and had a cookout with them. We also agreed to seek God's will about the possibility of holding some future ministry events together. It was a very blessed day, and we thanked God for our newfound friendship.

The next day, DQ and I stayed busy ministering to people. Just after lunch, three young people came and said they were hungry but had no money. Several churches had turned them away.

The churches in Sturgis stop all food and outreach ministry during the motorcycle event, saying they only want to help locals. What a shame, because they miss many opportunities for the kingdom.

DQ asked me if we had enough food to feed the two men and one woman, all in their early twenties. I knew we were pretty low on food and funds, but I told DQ that we could feed them beans, rice, and mixed vegetables. The young folks said that would be great. I told DQ he had forty-five minutes to witness to them as the rice cooked.

DQ learned that one of them had been raised as a Catholic, one as a Christian, and the other as an agnostic, yet each had many questions about God. By the time lunch was served, they commented that DQ made a lot of sense. They wondered why other Christians hadn't answered their questions so easily and in a way that made such sense. They took a Bible and promised to read it and pray that God would reveal Himself to them.

After they left, a woman came onto the property to talk to us. Her disheveled hair and dirty clothes revealed that she had been hard at work. She had tears in her eyes when she asked, "Do you have a Bible I can buy from you? I have ten dollars, but I've been run off by two churches and a funeral home. I just want a Bible!"

"It's all right," DQ told her. "I have a Bible you can have for free."

She said, "No. I want to pay you for it, so that it's mine. Here's a dollar. Thanks." Then she just turned and left with her Bible. DQ and I smiled at each other and thought it was all a little strange, but thanked Jesus we were there for her.

That evening as DQ, Pastor John, and I visited outside, she came back. We almost didn't recognize her, because she was clean and had on decent clothes. She introduced herself as Nora Jean. She explained that she worked for the carnival and had just gotten off work when she stopped by earlier. She said the difference between her and the rest of the carnies was that she realized how bad she was messing up. Nora Jean had been raised Southern Baptist and now felt Jesus calling her back to

Himself. We reminded her that He was right there where He had always been, but she had moved away from Him. The three of us prayed with her. Pastor John began and she finished. Nora Jean said she wanted to attend our church service, but would be gone in the morning, because the carnival was moving on. I connected her with a church in the town where she was headed, and the church was ready for her when she arrived. One more prodigal who came home to the Lord.

Chapter 30

Why Iowa, Lord?

God had led us very clearly when we left Florida for North Carolina, went back down to Gulfport, Mississippi, on to Texas, up through New Mexico and Colorado, and finally arrived at Sturgis, South Dakota. We weren't sure, though, where God wanted us to go from there. Since the tent ministry in Sturgis ended, we had been praying about where and when God wanted us to go next. Pastor John asked us every day when and where we were going, and our answer was always that God hadn't told us yet.

Our original plan (well, *my* original plan) was to head west into Montana and then on to the west coast. It seemed to us, though, that the Holy Spirit was blocking my desire. We had learned during our trip that every step we took was important, because God had a pathway of divine opportunities for us.

Our prayers were answered when the Holy Spirit told us to leave Saturday and head east to Iowa. I must admit that I was more than a little disappointed. Iowa? What's in Iowa except cornfields and small towns? I had never been out west, and that was where I wanted to go. God wasn't in as much of a hurry as

I was. He would have me wait twenty-four more years before I would ride the Pacific Coast Highway.

Unlike me, DQ was glad we were heading east. He had endured many worries on our journey, so it comforted him to be getting closer rather than farther away from home. We called our parents before we left. My mom and dad were glad we were heading back. It was hard being so far from them. I loved and missed them very much. DQ's mom made him feel guilty, as usual, but he had a decent talk with her. She said she was proud that he was an ordained minister, but wished he would pastor a church down the road from her and drive a red pickup truck instead of a red Harley-Davidson. That wasn't likely to happen. God's calling stood. Besides, I would make a horrible preacher's wife.

Travel days were long and hard. The bus bounced us around so much that we were hurting midway through the day. The day we left Sturgis, we made it as far as the Missouri River. The bus was slow. It averaged 50 mph, and that was on the flatland. Uphill was embarrassing sometimes. The Chamberlain, South Dakota rest stop was on a cliff overlooking the Missouri River. It was a magnificent sight. We walked the trails to stretch our legs, and then we had a couple of cans of cold veggies and some bread for supper.

We didn't sleep too well since the rest area was noisy, the weather was hot, and the inside of the bus was even hotter. We continued without air conditioning on the road, even though we had the generator. Freestanding generators, like ours, are very noisy compared to the built-in ones that motorhomes use. We spent the next night in a truck stop just inside the Iowa border. Surprisingly, it was quieter than the rest stop, so we got some sleep after we ate peanut butter and jelly sandwiches for dinner.

We had talked all the way from Sturgis about why God led us to Iowa. We didn't know anyone there and had no church or biker contacts. Even once we were in Iowa, we still didn't know what God had planned for us. We hoped to find a church that would let us stay until God led us on. I was reading our devotional and Bible study out loud as DQ drove, when he suddenly interrupted me by yelling, "Woo-Hoo! We know someone who lives in Iowa: Ray's ex, Cecily, and their son, Tom!" As the words came out of his mouth, I knew that was why we were there. We had no idea where in Iowa they lived, but we had Ray's number. We had reconnected with him and baptized him when we were in North Carolina.

We needed a place where we could make and receive phone calls that night when Ray would be off work. I looked in our *Directory of the Ministry* for a church in the area. I looked at the map, looked up, and said, "Pull off now! This is the exit with the church." DQ quickly pulled onto the exit ramp and geared down. Whiting Christian Church was three miles down the road.

Cecily, Ray, and Tom were old friends from North Carolina. We knew Ray long before we got saved. When they were younger and needed to get on their feet, we helped them out. In 1987, Ray called and asked if his little family could live with us in Orlando, Florida, while he went to the American Motorcycle Institute to become a Harley-Davidson mechanic. We welcomed them in. I helped Cecily get a job at the restaurant where I worked, and DQ even helped care for three-year-old Tom. Needless to say, we became close friends through it all. Ray was in school all day and Cecily worked different shifts. When Ray graduated, they moved back to North Carolina, where he got his dream job at a local Harley Davidson dealership. Sadly, after a few years, Ray and Cecily separated. All we knew was that Cecily and Tom had moved back to her hometown in Iowa.

We pulled into the church parking lot and DQ knocked on the church doors, but no one answered. Then he knocked on the door of the house next to the church. A man answered who identified himself as the pastor of the church. DQ introduced himself and told Pastor Shawn about our mission. Shawn and DQ got acquainted while we waited for Ray to get off work. It would be a gross understatement to say that we weren't what Pastor Shawn typically had in mind when he thought of missionaries. However, DQ was getting along well with him, and I was quickly getting to know and become friends with his wife, Suzie.

At the appointed time, I called Ray while DQ shared about our ministry with the men of the church. Ray was thrilled and blown away to hear from us, and he explained that he had been praying that God would have us call. Cecily and her fiancé were arrested the day before, and the powers that be had locked down all their assets. "They need you badly," Ray told me. "Cecily even called and asked me to send you. I told her you had no phone and that she should pray." Ray gave me their phone number and address. He couldn't get over the fact that he had asked God to have us call him, and we actually called. God hears and answers prayers. We were meant to be there to help.

I got off the phone and fell on my face before God, worshipping Him for His goodness and faithfulness. I asked for guidance to speak His words to Cecily. Then I got up and called her. Her fiancé, Henry, answered the phone. I asked to speak to Cecily since I didn't know Henry. She got on the phone, and as soon as she heard my voice, she started crying. She asked where we were and if we would come to see them. I told her where we were and that we would be there the next night, which made her cry even more. Cecily said they had little food, no money, and everyone was shunning them in their small town of 460 residents. Even her family was mad at them and wouldn't help. I prayed with her before hanging up and promised that we would soon be there.

The people of Whiting Christian Church wanted us to stay

with them longer, but we promised to return after Sturgis the following year. They sent us off with all kinds of goodies from the garden, two huge yard birds (they were chickens but the size of small turkeys), and a bit of money. At least for a while, we would have some good food to eat besides canned food. We thanked Jesus.

Henry and Cecily lived about seven hours southeast of where we were. Of course, it took us ten hours to get there, but we arrived that night. They waited up for us and wanted to talk, so we told them to put on the coffee pot. The story unfolded. Henry lived in his father's house. Cecily, Henry, little Tom, and the father lived on the main floor. Henry's brother, Ricky, lived in the basement. Ricky had sold cocaine out of the basement, but one of his last buyers was a Drug Enforcement Agency officer. That fateful night, the feds burst into the house in swat-style riot gear, broke down the doors, and arrested everyone. They called Cecily's aunt to take little Tom, so he would be safe, and wouldn't end up with Child Protective Services. The DEA froze their bank accounts, and the house became a crime scene. They had no money available to buy food or gasoline for work, and little Tom was still terrified that someone with guns was going to break down the door and take his Mommy away. The father put the house up as collateral and got them all out of jail, but the residents of the small town were snubbing them. Cecily's family was furious that she and Tom were living there instead of going back to North Carolina.

We listened to the whole story, and then we shared and prayed with the family. Henry's dad left when we interjected the Spirit of God into the conversation, but the rest of the family seemed happy and relieved we were there. We talked and prayed into the early hours of the morning, and then DQ and I went to the bus to crash. We prayed together for wisdom about what to do and say, because even though we wanted to help, we wouldn't condone selling drugs out of their house.

We stayed with them ten days. The money the Whiting church had given us provided the desperate family with groceries and a tankful of gas. We also spent time with little Tom, who was now eight years old. We took the whole group to church on Sunday, except for Henry's dad and brother. Later that week, DQ and I led Cecily, her cousin, her niece, and her nephew to the Lord Jesus. On the second Sunday we were there, they were all baptized in a pond. We had a tailgate party afterwards. Praise the Lord!

We found out that Henry and his dad were both angry at God over the death of Henry's older brother, Steve. Henry was fifteen when his brother, who was his hero, died. Henry told DQ that Steve was a dynamite Christian and God did wrong by taking him. When we heard that, DQ and I prayed for God to soften their hearts so they would hear the truth. One afternoon, Henry wanted DQ to go to the cemetery with him to see his brother's grave. DQ went.

When they got there, Henry wept over Steve's grave and then became angry. DQ told him, "Henry, you say Steve was a great Christian who even told you about the Lord. Well, do you believe Steve is in heaven? Do you want to see Steve again? The only way that's possible is if you get right with Jesus. You are mad at the wrong person. Satan comes to kill, steal, and destroy. God comes to heal and save. Steve is enjoying bliss with his Lord. Won't you join him?"

Henry looked at DQ wide-eyed and said, "No one has ever told me that before. I want to see him again, and I'm going to try to get better, but I'm not ready yet."

DQ reminded him that he needed Jesus' healing and couldn't trust in his own goodness. "You will never be ready to lay aside your anger and loss," DQ told him, "but Jesus will take them from you if you will allow Him back in your life." Henry rededicated his life to Christ several months later.

We were amazed and in awe at the way God used us there in that small Iowa town. I praised God for not allowing my will to send us west instead of east. Four people's eternity hinged on that one decision. It is humbling to realize how hard God works to line up situations and people for His kingdom work.

"Dear Father, let us always work for you and not against you. Let us be willing to accept our lot, whether it is glorious or mundane. Let us love the lost, the downtrodden, and the unlovely. Help us see people through Your eyes and not our own. In Jesus' precious name. Amen."

Chapter 31

Church Politics

Blessed are you when people insult you and per-secute you, and falsely say all kinds of evil against you because of Me. Rejoice and be glad, for your reward in heaven is great; for in the same way they persecuted the prophets who were before you.
(Matthew 5:11-12, NASB)

We went to the family's church Sunday morning. It was where Cecily's family had gone for ages. Their local church had no Sunday evening service, so we drove to the next town over to worship at the Church of Christ that night. They had just begun when we arrived, so we sat toward the rear with everyone else. The leader of the study asked us questions about our salvation and about our ministry. They spent the whole hour drilling us instead of singing praises to Jesus or teaching a Bible study. We found that strange, but figured they might not get many missionaries coming their way. As we stood outside and talked after the service, the minister's wife asked if we would speak to the teens on Wednesday night. We accepted and were excited to have the ministry opportunity.

Wednesday night found us at the youth minister's home. The senior pastor was there at first but left after we met Michael and Jean, the youth minister and his wife. I picked up some weird vibes from them. Jean seemed angry. I prayed that her anger wasn't directed at us, since we had just met her. Michael seemed uptight. We focused on the children and hoped that the apparent tension might work itself out. We were there for the youth, and we were going to give them our best. We talked to them about walking with Jesus instead of pursuing sex, drugs, and the world. We poured our hearts out as we told them how we had messed up our lives and hurt ourselves and others before we came to Jesus.

They sat quietly and listened to us for an hour, and then we let them ask questions. One youth said, "My mom is a junkie and leaves my brother and me alone a lot without food. What do I do?" Another one shared, "My parents are in prison and our foster mom beats us with a lash." Our hearts broke for the kids, but the parents we met at the church didn't seem to line up with what the kids were going through. We loved those kids and tried to point them in the right direction, right to Jesus Christ.

The van came to take them home. Michael and Jean invited us to stay for pizza. I drew Jean aside, asked her if she was all right and told her that I hoped we hadn't offended her. She said, "Mercy no! I'm not upset with you two. I'm furious and frustrated with the church leadership. You see, while you were here with the kids, they had a membership meeting debating your salvation and legitimacy."

I said, "That's okay, as long as we helped their kids."

Jean replied, "That's the other reason I'm livid. Those weren't our church kids. The church members wouldn't let you near their children. We picked up street kids and bussed them here. While I am glad the kids got to come, I'm upset about the others' self-righteous attitude." The whole scenario blew our minds, because we had no idea what had been going on. We had a great rest of the evening with Michael and Jean and assured them that God had the right children there. While we visited, the pastor called and canceled our planned dinner with him and his wife for the next evening. He told us something else had come up. We figured that their church meeting didn't go in our favor.

We've never courted men's favor and would rather have God's favor anytime.

Chapter 32

The Evil One's Fiery Darts

W e had ridden our motorcycles – DQ's 1971 Harley Davidson Shovel/Pan and my 1965 Triumph Bonneville – to our talk with the kids so they could see the bikes. When we cranked up the bikes for our ride back, we noticed that DQ's headlight wasn't very bright. Everything else seemed fine, so we began the 30-mile trip back to Henry and Cecily's house. About halfway back, DQ realized his bike was spewing oil. The oil had soaked through the cloth-wrapped wiring system and prevented his headlight from shining at all. We were on a two-lane road that cut through the cornfields, so the deer population was heavy. We couldn't stop in the middle of nowhere with no light and only a few tools, so we rode side-by-side and shared my bright headlight. As we rode, my hi-beam went out, but we could still see. To add to our adventure, we had no clear night glasses to wear, so the bugs were killing our eyes.

All of a sudden, my head ducked involuntarily, and as I glanced up, a bat bounced off my forehead. Had my guardian angel not pushed my head down, I would have been hit directly in the face, which could have knocked me out. As it was, I saw stars and let off the throttle. When I did that, DQ flew out in front of me into the dark. He shouted at me to get up there so he could see, and I shouted at him that I had just been hit by a bat. We were both trying to be heard, but our voices were drowned out by the roar of our bikes. Finally, I caught up with DQ, and we made it back. Our eyes looked like they were bleeding, and I had a big red mark on my forehead. What a ride! We were happy it was over, and we had another great story to tell.

Chapter 33

Opportunities in St. Louis

After ten days in Iowa, the Lord led us to check on a few friends we met and ministered to in Sturgis. We easily found Bob and Jazeen. They recommitted their lives to Christ at Sturgis, and we had performed their marriage ceremony. They seemed to be settling in well, and we were able to hook them up with a church in St. Louis.

We stayed at a church on the outer loop. The pastor, Dr. Peter, listened to our story and was very taken with our mission. He invited us to a pastor's meeting on Thursday, and we graciously accepted. Since we didn't look like the typical pastor's meeting attendees, we left many people speechless when we walked in. Each pastor, though, took a few minutes to introduce himself and share about his work in the area. After Dr. Peter spoke, he introduced us. We had both planned to take the podium, but the Spirit quenched me, so DQ went up alone. They were having a hard-enough time getting past the biker thing, so we didn't want to introduce the women thing to them too. DQ did a splendid job of sharing in love, and he won many of them over. We felt God had really gifted us in that area, because we often loved people past their prejudices on that tour. We were blown away that out of thirty pastors at the meeting, twenty-five took one of our brochures.

Over the next several days, we shared meals with a few different couples from the church. Each evening was a night of sweet fellowship and mutual challenges. People provided food, showers, laundry facilities, and meals for us. DQ and I were amazed and uplifted by the love the church poured out. We hated to leave at the end of the week, but we knew we would be back the next year for the North American Christian Convention, which was to be hosted in St. Louis, Missouri. We intended to have a booth at the convention.

Thank you, sweet Jesus, for brothers and sisters in Christ.

Chapter 34

Southern Hospitality

I was a stranger, and you invited Me in.
(Matthew 25:35 NASB)

At Daytona Bike Week, Mike had come to our first Sunday worship service. He was in Daytona with a painter named Jonathan. They had invited us to their hometown of Elizabethton, TN, on our way home so we could get to know each other better. Since our travels took us from St. Louis to Burlington, North Carolina, they were on our way, so we visited them.

We arrived in Elizabethton after five days of driving. It had been a long, hot five days, and we were glad to be somewhere where we could rest. It was pouring rain when we pulled into town. The gutters and ditches were full, and the water in the streets couldn't run off quickly enough. We came to a fork in the road, and I told DQ to go right. That choice led us directly to a convenience store two blocks down. DQ went inside and asked to use the phone. The owner looked him up and down and said, "There's a pay phone on the corner of the lot. Do you need quarters?" So DQ stood in the pouring rain and made phone calls using our *Directory of the Ministry* to try to find a church nearby.

It was Friday afternoon around four. No one was in any of the church offices. He started with the *A*'s and was on the *W*'s before he got an answer, all the while standing in the monsoon-like rain; poor dear. Finally, DQ heard, "Good afternoon, Westside Christian Church. How can we serve you?" DQ almost forgot what to say. He quickly recovered and asked for the senior minister, Jim Curtis. DQ explained our ministry and told Pastor Curtis that we were in town to follow up on some people we had met in March. He explained that we just needed some electricity to plug our bus into and maybe a few showers while we were there.

We would forever remember what he said, "Come on down, little buddy." Pastor Jim continued, "I have an appointment until five, so I will come meet and greet you then. I am so sorry I am tied up. Where are you?" DQ let him know where we were, and Jim laughed. He said, "You are only four blocks from the church! Ain't God good?" Little did any of us know that this short conversation would result in a multi-generational friendship.

While waiting for Jim Curtis to show up, we called our friends, Mike and Jonathan, to let them know we were in town. When Jim showed up a little after five o'clock, we realized that he was a gentle giant. He was over six feet tall, but soft-spoken. He loved Jesus, his family, his calling, and his people. He had called DQ "little buddy," before realizing that DQ was about ten inches shorter than him. The bus worked well for us, but poor Jim had to stoop over when he stood inside. So we fellowshipped in Jim's office instead of in the bus. Jim got us hooked up to electricity, but we still had no running water for the bus. He invited us over for dinner and showers the next night. After he left, we got down on our knees and thanked God for bringing us there. We just knew something special was about to happen, and we were right where we were supposed to be in God's plan.

The next morning, Jonathan knocked on the bus door at seven and woke us up. He apologized for coming so early, and told us that he was going to be working out of town and he wanted to see us before he left. He brought his new girlfriend, Julie, with him. We had been praying for a good woman for him since we met him in Daytona seven months earlier. She seemed like a very nice young lady. We thought she was a bit young for him, but who were we to say anything with our own fourteen-year age difference. Jonathan and Julie wanted to hear all about our trip. They were happy to hear of its success and promised to keep praying for us. It was a quick visit, but we all enjoyed it immensely.

Jim picked us up at five thirty for dinner. He and his wife, Helen, lived in the parsonage just up the hill from the church. Their son, Rusty, and daughter-in-law, Trish, were there as well. Helen had dinner on the table when we arrived, so we washed up and sat down. We were hungry. Jim offered the blessing to God, and we enjoyed our meal together. Helen proved to be an excellent cook. They all wanted to hear more about the ministry, so we happily told our tales. There was much laughter around the table, and we all had a wonderful time. Rusty and Trish said that they would like to come witness with us sometime, and we told them they were welcome anytime. The world provided opportunity for ministry 24/7/365. Jim offered for us to spend the night at his house, but we had to get back and take care of our little dog, Sporty. So he told us to call him if we needed anything. We didn't tell him we had no phone. After dinner, we took showers, and Jim took us home to our bus.

We weren't home long before Mike showed up. He gave us a big bear hug and sat in DQ's chair. The bus was a bit short for him too. He wanted to hear every detail of what had happened to us since Daytona, and we wanted to know all about how his first year walking with Christ had gone. He stayed until twelve thirty that evening. All of us shared about our adventures with Jesus. We had a most excellent night's sleep, refreshed with the love of our new and our not-so-new friends.

Chapter 35

Old Time Religion

Westside Christian Church had the look of a traditional church. The building was brick, and the steeple tower was white. The stairs that led to the foyer outside the sanctuary stood front and center. To the left of the steps, a large bell announced church and Sunday school. The church was nicely landscaped, and the parking lot reached to three sides of the church. Because it was such a traditional-looking building, it crossed my mind that the people might not accept us. Nevertheless, on Sunday morning, we climbed those stairs to find out just where we stood.

We had no reason to be concerned. Both Sunday school and church were wonderful. The folks couldn't have been more friendly and welcoming, even though we were in our leather, biker attire. Pastor Jim asked us stand up while he introduced us, then he gave us the opportunity to tell the congregation about Christian Riders Ministry. Jim was excited about our ministry and it showed. The time of worship was really good. The congregation sang old hymns with commitment and feeling. And Jim was amazing when he preached. He went from a soft-spoken man to a thundering prophet as he delivered God's Word with power and energy. We were challenged and motivated.

After the service, we talked and shared stories, meeting new folks who accepted us just like we belonged there. We made plans with several people who invited us for lunch or dinner at their homes. It was such a blessing to meet new friends and renew old friendships.

We have come to believe that the hardest part of being on the road is the lack of family and friends. At home, we always have long-time friends around to invite over or to go to their house for a cookout. We all need friends, but on the road, the best we can hope for is to connect with someone or see someone we met a couple months earlier. The deep bond isn't there, though, and unfortunately, many people can't handle our traveling type of lifestyle. They think they want to be our friends, but when we leave, they don't put forth the effort necessary to maintain the relationship. They don't call us or write to us in order to grow the friendship. It's just too hard for them. I think they put a high shine on what we do. Yes, being God's traveling servants is a great honor, but the road is often hard and lonely. Thankfully, DQ and I are best friends, which helps greatly. The Lord our God provides all that we need for life (2 Peter 1:3).

Chapter 36

Every Need

*And my God will fully supply your every need
according to his glorious riches in the Messiah Jesus.*
(Philippians 4:19 ISV)

DQ always teased me that there were three times when I was guaranteed to have a migraine: when I was having my lady time, when I was leaving my mom, and when I was going to visit Inez, his mama. Well, I had a migraine, and we were on the trail to Burlington, North Carolina, to see DQ's mama. His brother, Charlie, Charlie's wife Cindy, and their two daughters, Tiffany and Tamra, lived next door to Mama. I said my hellos upon arrival and returned to the dark, quiet, cool bus to try to sleep off the migraine, giving DQ some one-on-one time with his mama.

The next day, I was still a little weak, but the headache was mostly gone. While I rested, DQ worked on the carburetors on my Triumph. When he thought they were ready, he kick-started the Triumph to life. It ran well for a few minutes and then stalled. He went to kick it again, but the motor was seized up. When he told me, I felt defeated. All tour long, one thing after another happened to the bikes, and we had very little riding time. We were supposed to be motorcycle missionaries, but if we never rode, we couldn't make the impact that we desired and the bikers needed. Also, it seemed like we were always sinking money into our bikes. DQ said he would call his friend Stony that evening. Stony worked on British bikes and would be able to fix my Triumph. So DQ started to work on his own bike. Stony picked up my bike that evening but said it would be a couple of days before he would be able to see what was wrong with it.

At least we could borrow Inez's car, so we could go to Chapel Hill and see Alisha, DQ's daughter, my step-daughter. Stony called on Saturday, three days after he had picked up my bike. He told us that the oil pump on the Triumph had quit, locking up the bottom end. It would cost $400 to fix. We prayed that God would send the money. Our mail packet arrived the following Tuesday, and in it was a $418 real estate commission on a house I listed before we went into the ministry.

God is so awesome. We lack nothing that He deems we need. What a Father!

Since we left Sturgis where we saw the brand-new Harley Davidson Sportster for $4,775, we had been talking and praying about it. It was just so difficult to keep two old bikes running. We had paid more in repair bills every month than what payments on a new bike would be. After praying once more, we both had God's peace and knew it was His will for us to order the bike. We tried to sell the Triumph for the down payment, but had no takers.

DQ had always dealt with Durham Harley Davidson, so I called them and talked to our friend, who was the owner. He informed me that he had been allotted a black 883 Sportster for December, but that I could choose a different color for seventy-five dollars more. I chose a beautiful red color and told him that we would be down the next day to put a deposit on it. Our payments would be $132 a month, which was well worth it to have a running bike. I couldn't believe I was going to have my very own Harley. I was doing the happy dance all over town. I was very excited, and DQ enjoyed spoiling me, so he was grinning from ear to ear. It was going to be a long three months until December. Maybe the Harley would come in on my birthday, December 6. Thank you, Father. Thank you, Jesus. Thank you, Holy Spirit!

We picked up the Triumph from Stony, and I took it for a test drive. I pulled up to the stop sign at the end of the road, and the bike dumped all the oil out of the transmission. I really hated that bike at that point. It was cool looking, but I couldn't depend on it, and I was tired of it leaving us stranded. We called Stony when we got back to the house, but he had gone to the lake for the weekend. We originally planned to leave the next day, but because of this new setback, we wouldn't be able to leave until the following Tuesday or Wednesday.

It seemed that every time I returned to that town, I got stuck there. I longed to be gone. Everywhere I went, I felt like I had to watch my back. There were many people from my party days that I just didn't want to run into, but I had to come back. Our baby girl, Alisha, was there, as well as DQ's mama. I prayed, "Please, sweet Jesus, get me out of here!" I pouted for a while and DQ tried to cheer me up. I hated the Triumph and would be very glad to sell it as soon as it was fixed.

Chapter 37

The Hands of Time Go Round and Round

O n Sunday, we attended Burlington Christian Church. The service was good, and the minister was well spoken. Dick, the minister, talked to us after the service and asked DQ to speak to the congregation the next time we were in town. Dick said he would have to clear it with the elders first, but didn't think it would be a problem. We promised to stay in touch and let him know in advance when we planned to be back.

After church, we went to Chapel Hill to pick up Alisha and spend the day with her. It was the first day of the annual Carousel Festival at Burlington City Park. We were prayed up and ready to witness while there. The three of us strolled around, laughed, and had a great time. We rode the train together, something we hadn't done since Alisha was about three years old. DQ and I had as much fun that day as when we were teenagers.

It was there that we saw Gene "Bones" Boswell. Bones had been DQ's vice-president when we lived there six years before. He was always with DQ, always in the thick of it. When Bones saw us, he yelled, "Hey, I know you all, and I've been hearing some things about you both that I just will not believe! Is it true?"

DQ confirmed the rumor, "Yes, we have given our lives to Jesus Christ, and we now live to help others see Him through the darkness."

Bones turned his attention to me and said, "Not you too. I remember how bad you were."

I smiled and said, "Yes, Bones. Me too. Jesus has changed much about us, and we have finally found joy and peace."

Bones continued in astonishment, "But I know how low you two used to be! I can't believe someone as low as you can be where you are now."

DQ said, "See, He can change anyone!"

At that, Bones threw his hands in the air and said, "Good seeing you. Got to go." He mumbled until he faded back into the crowd, and we couldn't see or hear him anymore. We prayed for him right then.

We stayed at the park about two more hours. As we talked to folks, we saw Bones about six different times within earshot of us, watching and listening. We learned early on in ministry that there were always people watching to see if we were walking the walk. The real challenge is to be like Jesus when you think no one is watching. There is always someone watching.

We were overjoyed that we had run into Bones again. It was especially for the sake of our dear brothers and sisters that we had gone into the ministry. We knew that God would touch many people as we served Him, and we certainly didn't want those whom we loved to die and go to hell. We would see Bones again, though it would be many years before he would come to know Jesus. We never gave up on him or on the many others we used to run with.

We had been sharing Jesus with Alisha from the moment He changed our hearts and lives. On the way to take her home, to where she and Lyn, her mother, lived, we got into a deep spiritual conversation. As her daddy talked to her, the Lord laid on my heart that I needed to ask her for a decision that night. I prayed for gentleness, boldness, and wisdom to say the right words. We sat in the yard for some time after arriving at her home. Finally, I knew it was time, and I gently asked, "Honey, I know you pray and read your Bible, because you told us that, but do you have a personal relationship with Christ?"

She said, "I don't know. I think I do."

I asked, "Would you like to pray with us and make sure?"

Alisha smiled and said, "Yeah, I want to be sure."

We prayed right then and talked about what the Bible said about baptism.

She was baptized the next day in Durham, and God gave DQ the privilege of baptizing her. God's angels danced before His throne. As we drove the thirty minutes back to the bus, we cried tears of joy. We had failed Alisha many times by our past lifestyle, but we thanked Jesus for softening her heart, so she would want His peace and joy.

After that, I could rejoice in the breaking of the Triumph. Instead of leaving Saturday for Florida as we had intended, we had the opportunity to see Bones again and to be part of the greatest blessing ever with Alisha.

God's plans are often very different than ours. Thank you, Jesus, for guiding our lives and giving us the ability to choose your way each moment of every day.

Chapter 38

After Twenty-One
Weeks on the Road

We arrived back at our home church in Bayonet Point six days later than we thought we would, but were blessed because of what God had done. We were learning to trust in God's schedule rather than trying to force our own. We were very weary, but happy to be back. Our debriefing was scheduled for the next morning with Senior Minister Mel Gresham first and then with Associate Minister Michael Winsor. It would be great to see everyone and tell our stories. That first night in, though, we just wanted to sleep and relax, knowing we were home.

Our appointment with Mel Gresham was scheduled for 10:00 a.m. and with Michael Winsor for 11:00 a.m. DQ and I got up early and had our devotions. We were both excited to tell everything that God had done and what we learned while away. We really felt like we came back as different people. We met with Mel in his office and talked for about fifty minutes. We tried to cover everything that had happened on the road: the good, the bad, and the scary. Mel sat in his chair the whole time with a neutral face. When we finally stopped talking, he nodded his head and said, "I knew this year would either make you or break you. I am so thankful it has made you." He gave us some much-needed encouragement, and we scheduled our update to the congregation for a week later.

Then we met with Michael in his office. We began the same way, jabbering on about all the wild adventures God had seen us through. Michael cut us off around eleven thirty and asked questions which became increasingly more spiritual. He said that he couldn't believe the growth God had produced in us. We left as babies in the faith and came back as spiritual warriors. We left with an empty marriage and came back healed and united. We left worrying about everything and came back knowing that God had seen us through and would continue to do so. God had provided everything for us as we needed it, whether it was a tire changer in Pensacola or a train engineer in Colorado. He gave us new friends when we were lonely, and more importantly, He taught us to rely on each other.

Though we still had a long trail to maturity in Jesus Christ, our hearts were set on Him alone. We could no more stop following Jesus than we could stop the sun from rising. Christian Riders Ministry was established, and we were on fire for the Lord. The road had been long and hard in so many ways, but at our lowest point, God ignited us again and again. *When I say, "I won't remember the LORD, nor will I speak in his name anymore," then there is this burning fire in my heart. It is bound up in my bones, I grow weary of trying to hold it in, and I cannot do it!* (Jeremiah 20:9 ISV).

God, through Jesus Christ and the Holy Spirit, still had much more for us to learn and do, but that, readers, is for another time and another tale.

Meet the Author

Beth A. Mangus Roberts is the co-founder of Christian Riders Ministry. She is a missionary and nationally known inspirational speaker and biker. Her passion for Jesus is evident in all she does. She spends about 30 weeks a year on the road to attend motorcycle events as well as to speak at churches, retreats, and other events. When not traveling, she resides in North Carolina with her beloved Shetland Sheepdogs. Beth enjoys training and showing her dogs, as well as gardening and antiques.